endorsed for
BTEC

BTEC Level 2 Technical Certificate

Business Enterprise

Learner Handbook

Charlotte Bunn
Sue Donaldson
Claire Parry
Julie Smith

Pearson

Published by Pearson Education Limited, 80 Strand, London, WC2R 0RL.

www.pearsonschoolsandfecolleges.co.uk

Copies of official specifications for all Pearson qualifications may be found on the website: qualifications.pearson.com

Text © Pearson Education Ltd 2017
Typeset by Phoenix Photosetting, Chatham, Kent, UK
Original illustrations © Pearson Education Ltd 2017
Illustrated by Phoenix Photosetting, Chatham, Kent, UK
Picture research by Jane Smith
Cover photo/illustration © JAROON MAGNUCH / Shutterstock.com

The rights of Charlotte Bunn, Claire Parry, Julie Smith and Sue Donaldson to be identified as authors of this work have been asserted by them in accordance with the Copyright, Designs and Patents Act 1988.

First published 2017

22
10 9 8

British Library Cataloguing in Publication Data
A catalogue record for this book is available from the British Library

ISBN 978 1 292 19693 0

Acknowledgements
The author and publisher would like to thank the following individuals and organisations for permission to reproduce photographs:

(Key: b-bottom; c-centre; l-left; r-right; t-top)

123RF.com: 136, bayberry 9, kadmy 22, lightpoet 138, Markus Mainka 7, rh2010 34; Alamy Stock Photo: Angela Hampton Picture Library 71, Art Directors & TRIP 85, CandyAppleRed Signimage 55r, Chris Dorney 118, Cultura Creative (RF) 48, Diego Cervo 82, Emma Durnford 108, Hero Images Inc 139r, Ian Francis stock 68, keith morris 93r, Matthew Chattle 5, Peter Titmuss 91, REUTERS 16, Robert Clay 87, Stephen Barnes / UK 93c, Stuart Kelly 86r, WENN UK 89; Fotolia.com: Africa Studio 90, bernardbodo 116, foliavectorolirz 13, jack-sooksan 11b, kati_kapik 122, Monkey Business 142, Victor Moussa 8; Getty Images: sturti 67; Pearson Education Ltd: Gareth Boden 125, Jules Selmes 139b, Studio 8 126t; Shutterstock.com: Alexander Chaikin 109, dotshock 11c, DrimaFilm 32, Goodluz 139tl, Gyorgy Barna 98, hollandog 86l, Jacob Lund 27, JuliusKielaitis 93l, Lisa F. Young 28, mangostock 58, Matthew Williams-Ellis. 94, ofoto 18b, Paul J Martin 18t, Photobac 41, Ray Tang / REX 56, sursad 11t, Tupungato 55l, Vibe Images. 126b, wavebreakmedia ltd 144, Zadorozhnyi Viktor 36

All other images © Pearson Education

Contents

How to use this book

This handbook is designed to support you in developing the skills and knowledge to succeed in your BTEC Level 2 Technical course. It will help you to feel confident in taking the next step and to be ready for your dream job.

The skills you will develop during the course include practical skills that you'll need in your chosen occupation, as well as a range of 'transferable' skills and behaviours that will be useful for your own personal development, whatever you do in life.

Your learning can be seen as a journey which moves through four phases.

Phase 1	Phase 2	Phase 3	Phase 4
You are introduced to a topic or concept; you start to develop an awareness of what learning and skills are required.	You explore the topic or concept through different methods (e.g. watching or listening to a tutor or a professional at work, research, questioning, analysis, critical evaluation) and form your own understanding.	You apply your knowledge and skills to a practical task designed to demonstrate your understanding and skills.	You reflect on your learning, evaluate your efforts, identify gaps in your knowledge and look for ways to improve.

During each phase, you will use different learning strategies. As you go through your course, these strategies will be combined to help you secure the essential knowledge and skills.

This handbook has been written using similar learning principles, strategies and tools. It has been designed to support your learning journey, to give you control over your own learning and to equip you with the knowledge, understanding and tools to be successful in your future career or studies.

Getting to know the features

In this handbook you'll find lots of different features. They are there to help you learn about the topics in your course in different ways and to help you monitor and check your progress. Together these features help you:

- build your knowledge and technical skills
- understand how to succeed in your assessment
- link your learning to the workplace.

In addition, each individual feature has a specific purpose, designed to support important learning strategies. For example, some features will:

- get you to question assumptions around what you are learning
- make you think beyond what you are reading about
- help you make connections across your learning and across units
- draw comparisons between the theory you are learning about and realistic workplace environments

- help you develop some of the important skills you will need for the workplace, including planning and completing tasks, working with others, effective communication, adaptability and problem solving.

Features to build your knowledge and technical skills

Key terms

Terms highlighted LIKE THIS, are 'Key terms'. It is important that you know what they mean because they relate directly to your chosen subject. The first time they appear in the book they will be explained. If you see a highlighted Key term again after that and can't quite remember its definition, look in the Glossary towards the end of the book – they are all listed there! Note that these key terms are used and explained in the context of your specialist subject or the topic in which they appear, and are not necessarily the same definitions you would find in a dictionary.

Practise

These work-related tasks or activities will allow you to practise some of the technical or professional skills relating to the main content covered in each unit.

> **Practise**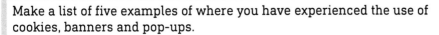
>
> Make a list of five examples of where you have experienced the use of cookies, banners and pop-ups.
>
> 1 What was the website promoting?
>
> 2 How effective was its promotional message? Did it make you want to buy the products or services?

Skills and knowledge check

Regular 'Skills and knowledge check' boxes will help you to keep on track with the knowledge and skills requirements for a unit. They will remind you to go back and refresh your knowledge if you haven't quite understood what you need to know or demonstrate. Tick off each one when you are confident you've nailed it.

> **Skills and knowledge check**
>
> ☐ What is meant by reflecting on your performance?
>
> ☐ Name the four focus points in a **SWOT ANALYSIS**.
>
> ☐ Suggest five headings that you might find in an action plan.
>
> ☐ Explain the difference between an open and a closed question.
>
> ○ I can evaluate information from a variety of sources.
>
> ○ I can give and receive constructive feedback effectively.
>
> ○ I can analyse data.
>
> ○ I can set personal targets.

What if...?

Employers need to know that you are responsible and that you understand the importance of what you are learning. These 'What if...?' scenarios will help you to understand the real links between theory and what happens in the workplace.

What if...?

Danny and Samil have been running their market stall selling CDs and DVDs since 2001. In recent years they have found that demand for their products has fallen and they are now struggling to make a living from the market stall. They have organised a meeting with a local business adviser to consider the options available.

1   How could Danny and Samil use the product life cycle to help them consider what is going wrong with their business?

2   What revision and development strategies could they introduce to help increase the number of customers visiting their market stall?

Link it up

Go to Unit 2 to find more information on the risks and benefits of innovation and USPs.

Link it up

Although your BTEC Level 2 Technical is made up of several units, common themes are explored from different perspectives across the whole of your course. Everything you learn and do during your course will help you in your final assessment. This kind of assessment is called 'synoptic'. It means that you have the opportunity to apply all the knowledge and skills from the course to a practical, realistic work situation or task.

The 'Link it up' features show where information overlaps between units or within the same unit, helping you to see where key points might support your final assessment or help you gain a deeper understanding of a topic.

Step-by-step

This practical feature gives step-by-step descriptions of processes or tasks, and might include a photo or artwork to illustrate each step. This will help you to understand the key stages in the process and help you to practise the process or technique yourself.

Checklist

These lists present information in a way that is helpful, practical and interactive. You can check off the items listed to ensure you think about each one individually, as well as how they relate to the topic as a collective list.

Features connected to your assessment

Your course is made up of several units. There are two different types of unit:

- externally assessed
- internally assessed.

The features that support you in preparing for assessment are below. But first, let's look at the difference between these two different types of unit.

Externally assessed units

These units give you the opportunity to present what you have learned in the unit in a different way. They can be challenging, but will really give you the opportunity to demonstrate your knowledge and understanding, or your skills, in a direct way. For these units you will complete a task, set by Pearson, in controlled conditions. This could take the form of an exam or onscreen test, or it could be another type of task. You may have the opportunity to research and prepare notes around a topic in advance, which can be used when completing the assessment.

Internally assessed units

Internally assessed units involve you completing a series of assignments or tasks, set and marked by your tutor. The assignments you complete could allow you to demonstrate your learning in a number of different ways, such as a report, a presentation, a video recording or observation statements of you completing a practical task. Whatever the method, you will need to make sure you have clear evidence of what you have achieved and how you did it.

Ready for assessment

You will find these features in units that are internally assessed. They include suggestions about what you could practise or focus on to complete the assignment for the unit. They also explain how to gather evidence for assessment from the workplace or from other tasks you have completed.

> ### Ready for assessment
>
> For your assignment, you will need to explain and evaluate the features of successful enterprise ideas.
>
> 1 Select two products or services that have been successful and explain which of the successful features they have, and how they have generated them.
>
> 2 Evaluate these features. This involves explaining which features have been most important and how much they have contributed to the overall success of the enterprise idea.
>
> 3 Analyse how the entrepreneurs behind these products and services have developed and implemented their enterprise ideas.
>
> 4 Identify the benefits and risks of enterprise. List these under each of the headings of 'Benefits of enterprise' and 'Risks of enterprise'. You can then use your list in your assignment work for this learning aim.
>
> 5 Now create your own idea for a product or service for a new business start-up. Explain the features that make it successful and their contribution to the start-up's success.
>
> | Benefits of enterprise | Risks of enterprise |
> |---|---|
> | | |

Assessment practice

These features include questions similar to the ones you'll find in your external assessment, so you can get some experience answering them. Each one relates to one or more Assessment Outcomes, as indicated in the top right-hand corner of this feature box. Suggested answers are available on our website, www.pearsonschoolsandfe.co.uk/BEanswers. Where Assessment practice features require you to carry out your own research or give individual answers or opinions, however, no answers are provided.

Getting ready for assessment

This section will help you to prepare for external assessment. It gives information about what to expect in the final assessment, as well as revision tips and practical advice on preparing for and sitting exams or a set task. It provides a series of sample questions and answers that you might find, including helpful feedback, or 'verdicts', on the answers and how they could be improved.

Features which link your learning with the workplace

Work focus

Each unit ends with a 'Work focus' section which links the learning from the unit to particular skills and behaviours that are required in the workplace. There are two parts in each Work focus section:

1. **Hands on** – gives suggestions for tasks you could practise to develop the technical or professional skills you'll need on the job.
2. **Ready for work?** – supports you in developing the all-important transferable skills and behaviours that employers are looking for, such as adaptability, problem solving, communication or teamwork. It will give you pointers for showcasing your skills to a potential employer.

HANDS ON

Problem solving is an important part of working life. In business you will come across a range of issues that need attention.

- Identify problems you can solve without requiring you to analyse your actions.

- Identify practical problems that simply require you to learn through practice or repetition. For example:

  - the technology is not working for your presentation
  - you have arrived at a venue to do a pitch and you have been given the wrong date
  - correcting errors in written work
  - computer problems.

- If possible, direct the problem to the relevant person who has responsibility for that working area (for example the Technical Department).

- Remember that it is not failure to ask for help.

- With difficult problems, work through a process:

  - identify the problem
  - describe the problem
  - explain issues within the problem
  - ask relevant questions to clarify information given
  - make realistic and appropriate decisions that will help to solve the problem
  - come up with creative and innovative ideas to solve the problem
  - show resolve and resilience in solving the problem.

- Develop your **BUSINESS ACUMEN** (a clear understanding of how your business works):

  - can be developed over time, because knowledge of working practices grows through experience
  - helps with problem solving and dealing with complex issues.

Ready for work?

Do this short quiz to find out whether you would make a successful entrepreneur.

1 On deciding what enterprise idea to choose, you should:

☐ A Develop all the options and then decide.

☐ B Focus on one idea and develop it.

☐ C Ask other people's opinions on each idea before deciding.

☐ D Pick the first idea you come up with.

2 When refining an enterprise idea, you should:

☐ A Consider the strengths and weaknesses of the idea.

☐ B Look at what was good and ignore the rest.

☐ C Use creativity techniques to reassess and refine the idea.

☐ D Go with the idea anyway because you think it is a good idea.

3 When undertaking secondary research:

☐ A Use a range of websites checking they are correct.

☐ B Use the websites of businesses you know a lot about.

☐ C Use a number of sources to double-check the information is correct.

☐ D Use the first website you come across.

4 When using primary research, it is important to:

☐ A Use a range of techniques to make sure the information is accurate.

☐ B Ask your friends and family for their opinions.

☐ C Think carefully about selecting the right people to match the target market.

☐ D Write down your own opinions, because you know what people think.

5 When presenting your ideas and research:

☐ A Make notes under key headings with your reasons for the decisions you made.

☐ B Outline the enterprise idea and explain why you think it will work.

☐ C Produce a detailed, professionally presented report.

☐ D Write down the decision made and your reasons for it.

Your score:

A = 2; B = 3; C = 4; D = 1

If you scored mostly As, you may need to brush up on your enterprise skills. Mostly Bs, go back and read the relevant learning aim of the unit. Mostly Cs, you have a good understanding of the skills involved. Mostly Ds, you need to revisit the content in this unit.

1 The Business Enterprise Environment

Trying to run a successful business would be difficult if you did not satisfy your customers by selling them products and services that they want and need.

In this unit you will learn the characteristics and factors that make entrepreneurs and enterprises successful in the business environment. It will give you the core knowledge and understanding for developing enterprise skills in small to medium-sized enterprises.

How will I be assessed?

In this unit you will be assessed using an onscreen test that is set and marked by Pearson.

You will need to know the features of different enterprises, how the operational environment may impact businesses and what affects the success of enterprises. You will then consider a number of case-study business enterprise scenarios.

Assessment outcomes

AO1 Demonstrate knowledge and recall of business and enterprise principles, key terms and definitions
Command words: complete, explain, give, identify, match, name, outline, state
Marks: range from 1 to 2 marks

AO2 Demonstrate understanding and application of business and enterprise concepts, financial processes, features and data sources relating to business enterprise success factors, business organisations and the environment in which they operate, and the role of enterprise and innovation
Command words: calculate, complete, explain, identify, outline
Marks: range from 1 to 5 marks

AO3 Be able to assess or analyse business information and data, demonstrating the ability to identify and compare relevant information or data, make connections, predict probable consequences and provide reasonable alternatives
Command words: analyse, assess, discuss, explain
Marks: range from 1 to 6 marks

AO4 Be able to evaluate or assess business and finance information and data suggesting/providing solutions and making informed judgements, including synthesising ideas and evidence from several sources to support arguments and form conclusions
Command words: assess, discuss, evaluate, explain
Marks: range from 1 to 6 marks

What you will learn in this unit:

A   The features of different enterprises

B   Impact of the environment on the success of an enterprise

C   The contribution of enterprise to business success

D   Business enterprise ideas

A The features of different enterprises

A1 Ownership, liability and size

Walmart and McDonald's employ millions of people. But many **ENTERPRISES** are one-person businesses such as local plumbers and electricians. McDonald's is a private business, run for profit. But some enterprises, such as the BBC, are public-sector businesses. Other businesses, such as Co-op Food and Divine Chocolate, are set up for social purposes. Choices that a business makes between different types of ownership, **LIABILITY** (whether or not the owner of a business is personally responsible for its debts) and the size of operations has important impacts on its success.

Practise

List the different types of enterprises in your local area.

1 How many people do you think own each enterprise?

2 Do you think the owners would lose their house if the enterprise failed?

3 How many people work for each enterprise?

Ownership

One of the first decisions an **ENTREPRENEUR** – someone who starts a business – should make when setting up an enterprise is how it is going to be owned. There are several different types of ownership of an enterprise.

Private sector enterprises

Most businesses are in the **PRIVATE SECTOR** (the part of the economy run by private individuals or organisations, rather than the state). These include John Lewis, River Island, Tesco and Virgin Atlantic. But they can also include local plumbers and electricians. The type of ownership within the private sector can vary greatly.

Sole trader

Many enterprises in the UK are **SOLE TRADERS**. These are 'one-person' businesses, commonly known as being self-employed, such as small shop owners and taxi drivers.

This type of ownership is available to anybody who has an idea and wants to start their own enterprise. Charities such as The Prince's Trust offer grants to young people starting their own business. Many sole traders operate in their local area. Some might also operate nationally and internationally, often through the internet.

Table 1.1: Advantages and disadvantages of setting up as a sole trader

Advantages	Disadvantages
• Easy to set up – no forms or procedures • Owner keeps all profits • Owner has control of the business and makes all decisions • Owner is flexible to run the business how they want, and take holidays when they want • Thanks to the internet, sole traders can even operate nationally and internationally	• Has **UNLIMITED LIABILITY**. This means that the owner is personally responsible for any debts that the business has and may have to sell personal belongings to pay these off. • If the owner has no employees, the business may need to close if they are ill or on holiday, so may lead to debt due to not generating **REVENUE** (the money a business makes from sales), and loss of customers. • If a dispute arises, the owner could be sued. • The owner may not have all the necessary skills to run a business. Having to hire others with these skills is a cost to the business.

Assessment practice — AO2

James wants to start his own business. He is looking to create and sell apps at his college that will help learners with their coursework. The app is ready to be sold but he does not know how to go about starting the business. He gets advice from the Prince's Trust and his mentor. He goes to many college fairs and does a great deal of marketing, and begins to sell some of his apps. Soon he makes enough money to open a pop-up shop. He is very busy, starting work at 7.30 a.m. In the evenings, he comes up with new apps and offers to attract customers.

Explain to James the advantages of being a sole trader. (4 marks)

Partnership

PARTNERSHIPS are set up by two or more people, usually by professionals such as dentists, vets and accountants. Some of the world's largest businesses started out as a partnership, such as eBay, Apple and Twitter.

Partners can share some of the business decision making, and need to agree on aspects such as:

- how the profits will be shared
- how much a partner will need to invest in the business
- what each partner will need to do in the business
- how they would recruit a new partner and get rid of one they no longer wanted.

Limited liability partnerships

There are two different types of partnership: a **LIMITED LIABILITY PARTNERSHIP** (LLP) and a limited partnership. In an LLP, partners are not liable for any debts the business cannot pay. In a limited partnership, partners can sometimes be liable for debts.

Table 1.2: Advantages and disadvantages of setting up a partnership

Advantages	Disadvantages
• Easier to expand than a sole trader because they could take on a partner who has the necessary expertise. • Extra **CAPITAL** (the money, buildings and equipment used to run a business) – the more partners there are, the more money is invested into the business. • Partners share the workload and decision making. • Partners can take holidays and let the other partners run the business while they are away. • In an LLP, partners have limited liability for any debts the partnership cannot pay.	• In a limited partnership, some partners can be personally responsible for any debts that the business has and may have to sell personal belongings to pay these off. If they cannot pay off these debts, they may become **INSOLVENT** (unable to pay their debts). • Partners may disagree on decisions that need to be made or how the business should be run. • Profits are shared between partners.

Assessment practice   A02

Imogen is a sole trader. She owns a hairdressing salon. She wants to expand her business and is considering forming a partnership with her brother, Harry.

Explain to Imogen the advantages of her business becoming a partnership. (4 marks)

Many enterprises start out as a sole trader or partnership. When the enterprise is doing well and they want to expand, the owners often find that they do not have enough money on their own to invest into the business to make the expansion possible. In addition, if they are a sole trader, they must accept unlimited liability, which means every decision has an added risk. The solution to this is becoming a **LIMITED LIABILITY** company, which means that investors can put money into the company, but without the risk of unlimited liability.

It is also easier to attract investment, as it is easier for investors to come and go in a limited company than it is under other types of enterprise ownership. It is also more straightforward to sell the company on when partners are not involved. There are two types of limited company: **PRIVATE LIMITED COMPANY (LTD)** and **PUBLIC LIMITED COMPANY (PLC)**.

Private limited company (Ltd)

Private limited companies are usually small to medium in size and usually employ people other than the owners.

Private limited companies often have the abbreviation 'Ltd' after the company name when written in full, such as 'JCB Ltd'. They are often owned by friends and family, and each owner buys shares in the business to become a shareholder. A **SHARE** is a small piece of a business, which is exchanged for investing money into the business.

They usually operate on a regional scale, but national companies include Virgin Atlantic, New Look and River Island. This means that they usually have more customers, are more well-known and have higher sales.

Virgin Atlantic is one of the largest private limited companies in the UK (by sales volume)

Table 1.3: Advantages and disadvantages of setting up as a limited company

Advantages	Disadvantages
• Owners have limited liability. If the business fails, the shareholders can only lose the value of the shares that they have bought, not their own money. • Shareholders have tight control over who buys the shares. • The company can raise extra capital by selling more shares. • They usually have greater revenue than that of a sole trader.	• Each year the business must produce a set of financial accounts that must be checked by an independent accountant, which are then sent to Companies House. Small companies may submit abbreviated annual accounts to Companies House, which means less financial information is made available to the public. • Shares cannot be sold to the public. They are only bought by a few people. Every time shares are sold, all the existing shareholders must agree. • They are more expensive to set up than a sole trader enterprise or a partnership. • Profits have to be shared with the other shareholders.

Public limited company (plc)

Public limited companies are usually **LARGE ENTERPRISES**. They tend to employ thousands of people and make large profits. Their full company names include the abbreviation 'plc', such as 'Barclays Bank plc'. Other well-known public limited companies include Burberry and British Petroleum (BP).

Shares in a plc are bought and sold on the stock exchange at a particular price. You can find these prices in any major newspaper or online at www. londonstockexchange.com – the official website for the London Stock Exchange.

Table 1.4: Advantages and disadvantages of setting up as a public limited company

Advantages	Disadvantages
• Owners have limited liability. If the business fails, the shareholders can only lose the value of the shares that they have bought, not their own possessions. • Shares are bought by the public. The enterprise can raise extra capital by selling more shares. • Banks are more willing to lend the enterprise money. • If the business does well, the shares will increase in value, therefore the overall value of the company will also increase. • Some of the profit, after tax, can be paid to the shareholders as **DIVIDENDS** (a payment of money by a company to its shareholders, usually on a regular basis).	• Each year the business must produce a report and accounts. These can also be seen by competitors. • An annual general meeting must be held every year. • They are expensive to set up, as there are more rules and regulations to follow. • Profits are shared among all shareholders. • If the value of the shares fall, shareholders may sell their shares, which means that the business's value will fall further.

The London Stock Exchange is where shares are bought and sold for public limited companies

Assessment practice   A02

Steven owns an accounting firm with his partner Vejay. Steven and Vejay want to expand the business and are considering becoming a private limited company.

Assess the impact of Steven and Vejay's business becoming a private limited company. (6 marks)

Co-operatives

A **CO-OPERATIVE** is usually formed when a group of people come together to work towards a common goal. Co-operatives are owned and run by their members, whether those members are the employees, customers, local residents or suppliers. Two well-known co-operatives in the UK are Co-op Food (part of the Co-operative Group) and John Lewis:

The Co-operative Group is owned by its individual members and other co-ops. When there is a profit left over after it has been re-invested in the business, the members may get a dividend. The John Lewis Partnership is an employee co-operative. Its employees own John Lewis stores and Waitrose supermarkets. At its annual general meeting, its directors decide how much profit they will re-invest in the business and how much of a bonus can be paid out to its employees.

Advantages	Disadvantages
• Members have an input into the decision making of the firm and this can be very motivating and inspiring. • There tends to be more focus on ethics and customer service. • Certain customers may prefer to buy goods or services from a co-operative than from a more profit-orientated enterprise, particularly if they can become members of the co-operative and gain discounts.	• There are a lot of people to consider when making decisions and this may make it hard to make tough decisions, such as staff redundancies. • All members share the profits, even if most of the hard work is done by a small group of people.

Table 1.5: Advantages and disadvantages of setting up as a co-operative

John Lewis and the Co-operative Group are the UK's largest co-operatives

Public sector enterprises

PUBLIC SECTOR enterprises are owned and run, either fully or partly, by the government. They usually provide a service to a community. They are funded primarily with money provided by the government (either locally or nationally) through taxation (paid by taxpayers).

- *Government departments*, such as the Department of Health, provide funding to local areas to run services.
- **PUBLIC CORPORATIONS** include the BBC (which is funded through the payment of a TV licence) and the Civil Aviation Authority.

Not-for-profit enterprises

NOT-FOR-PROFIT enterprises are formed to pursue a goal that is not for the benefit of the organisation, sometimes providing products and services free of charge to further a social cause. One example of this is the NHS. Not-for-profit enterprises can be in the public sector or the private sector. Not-for-profits are funded by money they receive as donations from the government or public, or generated from sales.

- **CHARITABLE TRUSTS** are organisations created with the purpose of being charitable to others and benefiting the public. For example, Sainsbury's has a charitable trust that provides grants to registered charities.
- **VOLUNTARY SECTOR BUSINESSES** provide services or promote a cause that benefits the public. In some instances its staff work for free (voluntarily), but a large organisation will usually have paid staff too.
- **COMMUNITY INTEREST COMPANIES (CIC)** aim to use their profits for good causes. These are a special type of limited company that exists to benefit the community, instead of shareholders. For example, the Timewise Foundation is a CIC whose purpose is to get mothers back to work and help employers find experienced part-time employees.

Liability

In addition to ownership, the type of liability (whether it is limited or unlimited) can also affect the success of a business.

Table 1.6: Advantages and disadvantages of limited and unlimited liability

Liability	Advantages	Disadvantages
Limited	• The most the business owner can lose is the amount they invested in the business. This protects the personal wealth of the business owner. • Easier to raise finance from the selling of their shares and banks are more likely to lend the business money. • Can be more stable as the business can continue to operate even if the shareholders change.	• Have to disclose company information to Companies House. • Directors have legal duties as outlined in the Companies Act 2006.
Unlimited	• Do not have to disclose company information to Companies House, keeping business accounts off public records. • Moving capital and returning capital to shareholders is much easier than it is for limited companies.	• The owner or shareholders are personally responsible for paying business debts. • Failing to pay these debts may mean the owner is declared bankrupt.

Size

As well as ownership and liability, the size of a business will also have an impact on it.

- **MICRO** enterprises have up to nine staff. They will usually be sole traders, partnerships or private limited companies.
- **SMES** are small to medium-sized enterprises. Small enterprises have between 10 and 49 staff. Medium enterprises have between 50 and 249 staff.
- *Large enterprises* have more than 250 employees. Examples are the NHS, Chelsea Football Club and Facebook.

Assessment practice   A01

A business employs 150 staff.

What is the term used for this size of business? (1 mark)

Select *one* option:

☐ Micro

☐ Medium enterprise

☐ Small enterprise

☐ Large

A2 Purposes, sectors and scope

The purpose, sector and scope of an enterprise also affects how successful it will be.

Purpose

Enterprises exist for different reasons. The main purpose of most is to supply services or products. Some do this to make profit (for-profit businesses).

But not-for-profit businesses and organisations re-invest all their revenues to help the community.

Primary sector

Sector

Enterprises operate in four sectors of the economy:

1. The **PRIMARY SECTOR** is where raw materials are extracted and food is grown. Examples include farming and mining. This is the first stage of production, as businesses in this sector create resources that are then used by other businesses.

2. The **SECONDARY SECTOR** then uses the raw materials from the primary sector to transform these into products that are ready to be sold, for example car manufacturers.

3. The **TERTIARY SECTOR** provides services such as transport, education and retail, with retail being probably the largest part of this sector in the UK. This is where the products, transformed in the secondary sector, are sold to customers.

4. The **QUATERNARY SECTOR** provides information services to customers, such as information technology, consultancy, and research and development. This sector is growing quickly as more businesses invest in larger research facilities and IT. Jobs in this sector are highly skilled.

Secondary sector

Tertiary sector

Cotton is farmed to create clothes that are then sold in shops

Scope of business activities

The scope of an enterprise means the area it operates in.

- *Local* sole traders and partnerships operate in the areas they are based in geographically. They are likely to have customers within a 20-mile radius of their business, for example your local hairdresser or dentist.
- *National* businesses operate across the country. They are usually larger than local businesses and may be private limited companies and public limited companies, for example B&Q and Peacocks.
- *International* businesses operate in many countries around the world. Many public limited companies are international, such as Tesco and Primark.

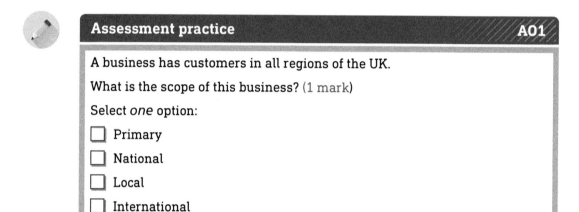

Assessment practice   **AO1**

A business has customers in all regions of the UK.

What is the scope of this business? (1 mark)

Select *one* option:

- ☐ Primary
- ☐ National
- ☐ Local
- ☐ International

Reasons for business success

There are many different reasons why some businesses are successful and others are not.

- *Strong customer service* is one of the reasons that John Lewis is so successful and the reason why many of its customers purchase products and services from it. Good customer service may mean that a business offers a favourable returns or exchange policy or free delivery.
- *Clarity of vision* means that the owners and employees of the business ensure that they have a clear idea of what they want the business to achieve. This can often mean being resilient and never giving up.
- Having *innovative products or processes* means finding a solution to a problem by creating or changing a product or service and this often means they are successful. For example, Phil Mundy was on a skiing holiday and found he couldn't use his touchscreen device when he was in the chairlift, as he had his ski gloves on. He invented iPrints, which are adhesive strips that you stick onto your gloves that allow you to use your touchscreen device without the need to remove your gloves. He now has a successful enterprise due to this innovation.
- *Meeting customer needs* is important to the success of a business, because if these are not met, customers may buy from competitors instead. For example, early MP3 players were very innovative, but were often quite complicated to use and time consuming to load music onto. Apple's iPod quickly became the biggest-selling MP3 player, when it launched in 2001, partly because it was so easy to use.

Forms of enterprise businesses

When an entrepreneur decides to set up their own enterprise business, there are different formats that they can choose.

- **START-UPS** are new businesses and are often small. The UK government is trying to encourage more start-ups as this helps the economy thrive. Launching a start-up means that the entrepreneur can give more choice to the public, earn an **INCOME** and help to keep prices low as there is more competition in the market. Income is the cash generated by a business – the costs taken away from the revenue.
- **LIFESTYLE BUSINESSES** are set up to provide the founder with enough income to enjoy the quality of life they desire and provide flexibility.
- **SOCIAL ENTERPRISES** are set up to tackle social problems, or to improve people's lives or the environment. They sell products and services but then reinvest most of the revenues they generate back into the business or the local community. Divine Chocolate is a social enterprise that is around 45 per cent owned by the cocoa providers who therefore get a better deal from the cocoa they sell and can invest this revenue back into their community.
- **FRANCHISES** are set up when the owner (franchisor) allows other people (franchisees) to use the name and the branding of an established business to set up a business of their own, effectively becoming an agent. The franchise must pay a fee and usually has to share the profits with the franchisor. Well-known examples are Domino's Pizza and Subway.

Social enterprises such as Divine Chocolate ensure that cocoa farmers get a better deal for the cocoa farmed and this revenue can then be re-invested into the community

Assessment practice AO1

Luisa left university and wanted a career as a travel writer. She soon realised this job was virtually impossible, but her heart was set on travelling, managing her own future and earning enough money to sustain this way of life. She now combines writing, teaching and managing a band, and this allows her the flexibility to travel and work.

Which form of enterprise is this? (1 mark)

Select *one* option.

- ☐ Lifestyle
- ☐ Social
- ☐ Franchise
- ☐ Start-up

A3 Stakeholders and their influence

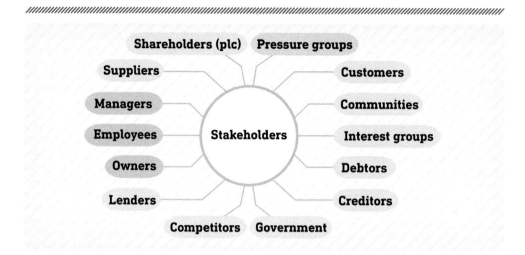

Figure 1.1: Some stakeholders will be external and some will be internal

Stakeholders

STAKEHOLDERS are the people, or groups of people, who are directly affected by, or have an interest in, a business. Some stakeholders have more influence than others.

Internal stakeholders

Internal stakeholders work inside the business. These include senior managers, employees and owners.

Table 1.7: Internal stakeholders

Position in the business	Role
Junior staff	• Work for the business • Seek job security, promotion opportunities and fair pay • Have a lot of influence that can make the business change its aims and objectives to include employees' needs and wants, such as better working conditions
Managers	• Work for the business • Manage the performance of more junior employees • Often act as a bridge between a business's owners and more junior staff • Have a lot of influence that can make the business change its aims and objectives, particularly if they are closely involved in operations
Owners	• If there is high unemployment, employers are in a more powerful position because jobs are harder to find • Have the most time and money invested in the business • Want to earn large profits • Have direct influence on the aims and objectives of the business and can influence it to make higher profits through expansion or growth

External stakeholders

External stakeholders work outside the business. These include shareholders, suppliers and lenders.

Table 1.8: External stakeholders

Role	Relationship to the business	Influence
Shareholders (in a plc)	• People or organisations that own a proportion (share) of the business. • Have the most time and money invested in the business. • Want to see large profits to increase their dividends.	Directly influence the aims and objectives of the business and can influence it to make higher profits through expansion and growth.
Suppliers	• Individuals or other businesses that provide products or services to the business. If multiple suppliers exist, a supplier can be replaced with one that has lower prices/rates. • They want large and regular contracts with selected businesses and to build close and long-lasting relationships. • If the business does not treat its suppliers well, for example by never paying them on time, it can damage its relationship with them.	Their influence can be high if there are a limited number of suppliers for a specific product/service. It is low if there are many suppliers.

Lenders	• Individuals or organisations that lend money to the business. These could be:
	  ○ financial institutions – for example, banks
	  ○ **VENTURE CAPITALISTS** – investors that provide either capital or support to start-ups, for a stake in the business – they often bring contacts and experience
	  ○ **BUSINESS ANGELS** – people who will take shares in your business in return for providing funds, as was the case with smoothie creator Innocent, which raised funding from business angels.
		Their influence depends on how much money has been lent to the business, as they will want the business to succeed to ensure they are paid back (often with interest) or for a share of the profits.

Competitors	• Businesses that sell similar products and services to other businesses. • They want to gain customers from other businesses to increase their market share and profits.	A business's competition should always be considered and will greatly influence its overall performance.
DEBTORS (also called trade receivables)	• People or organisations that owe the business money.	If debtors do not pay their debt to the business, this can affect whether the business has enough money to continue trading.
CREDITORS (also called trade payables)	• People or organisations that the business owes money to. • If they are not paid, they may not continue to supply the business, which could see the business becoming insolvent and having to stop trading.	Their influence has a greater impact if they stop supplying the business, possibly leading to insolvency.
Customers	• People, or organisations, who purchase products or services from the business. • Often driven by price, quality and value for money.	Have a large influence over the business because they can stop buying its products or services.
Government agencies and departments	• They want businesses to provide jobs and tax revenue, and help the economy grow. • These could be local (such as parking regulations and council tax on business premises), national (such as taxation and employment laws) or international (such as trade agreements).	Have little direct influence on how a private business is run. However, through taxation, support and employment laws, they have a strong influence on how a business behaves.
Communities	• People in the local community often want jobs and to minimise pollution and damage to the area. • National communities may be more interested in the tax revenues that a business generates. • International communities may have concerns about a business's impact on globalisation, such as climate change and exploitation of workers in less economically developed countries.	If the business behaves badly, communities can often bring about negative press coverage, so they must always be considered by the business.
Pressure groups and interest groups	• Groups of people or organisations that want to raise awareness of an issue and put pressure on businesses to act responsibly. • Often attract vast media attention.	Businesses need to listen to them because bad public opinion could have a huge impact on sales.

Pressure groups are stakeholders that enterprises must consider

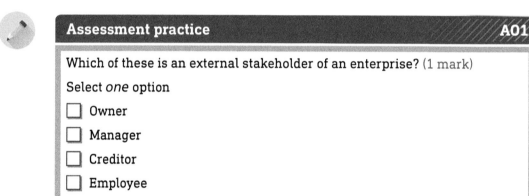

Assessment practice — A01

Which of these is an external stakeholder of an enterprise? (1 mark)

Select *one* option

- ☐ Owner
- ☐ Manager
- ☐ Creditor
- ☐ Employee

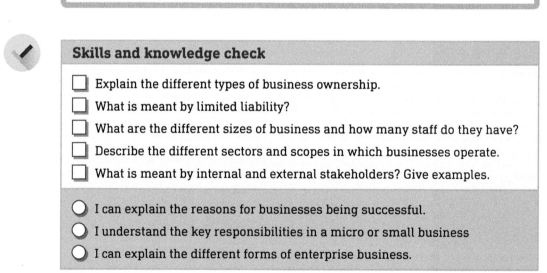

Skills and knowledge check

- ☐ Explain the different types of business ownership.
- ☐ What is meant by limited liability?
- ☐ What are the different sizes of business and how many staff do they have?
- ☐ Describe the different sectors and scopes in which businesses operate.
- ☐ What is meant by internal and external stakeholders? Give examples.

- ◯ I can explain the reasons for businesses being successful.
- ◯ I understand the key responsibilities in a micro or small business
- ◯ I can explain the different forms of enterprise business.

B Impact of the environment on the success of an enterprise

B1 The operational environment

The environment an enterprise operates in, or the **OPERATIONAL ENVIRONMENT**, can have a big impact on its success. Businesses must continually evaluate the internal (inside the business) and external (outside the business) factors that could affect their success and consider how they will overcome any obstacles, or grab any opportunities.

Political and economic

Political and economic factors that can have an impact on the success of an enterprise include everything from taxation levels to inflation.

Government support

Support from the government can take the form of:

- *Government spending and taxes*: the UK government has decided to spend a large amount on the development of HS2, the high-speed train that will eventually travel from London to Leeds and Manchester. So new enterprises may be set up to meet demand for this development. But this can also increase competition for existing enterprises.
- *Government initiatives*: the government's New Enterprise Allowance encourages people on benefits to start their own business. This is an example of a government initiative that helps enterprises to start up.

Inflation

Inflation is the term for the price of products and services rising. This can affect enterprises because the more prices increase, the less spending power customers have as products and services become more expensive. Businesses may start losing customers, which means fewer sales and less profits. Businesses may then start making people redundant. As living costs rise, businesses are then under pressure to increase the wages that they pay to their staff, which is another cost for businesses.

Sources of finance available to new ventures

If inflation rises, and businesses see their profits fall and wage bill rise, the economy starts to shrink as less people have money to spend. Banks won't want to lend as much money to new enterprises as they are unsure that the enterprises will be able to pay the money back.

Social

There are several social factors that can have an impact on the success of an enterprise.

Major engineering projects, like new high-speed rail lines, can bring opportunities for new enterprises

People's attitudes to saving, spending and debt

The general public's attitude to spending can impact the success of an enterprise. If people are more willing to spend their money or indeed borrow money (for example using credit cards or taking out loans), rather than save it, it will mean they are more likely to purchase goods and services. Therefore enterprises will make more sales. If people are more inclined to save money than to spend it, businesses can have a harder time bringing in enough income.

Changes in population trends

DEMOGRAPHICS are the characteristics of human populations, for example the average age of a group of people. It is important that businesses know how demographics change, so that they can make products or services (or indeed stop selling some products or services) that appeal to the demographics of their customers. As people are living longer, some businesses have started tapping into this new market. Nintendo Wii, for example was originally developed for young gamers. However, since then it has developed games that appeal to older people, for example Wii Fit Plus and Big Brain Academy.

Social responsibility requirements

People nowadays are far more aware of their social responsibility to do good. Many people use social media and are, therefore, more exposed to social issues that are happening around the world. Businesses have become aware of this and now support more social issues than ever before in the hope that people will make purchases from them to support these causes.

Changes in consumers' tastes/preferences

The increasing awareness of our health and fitness has meant that more gyms and personal training enterprises have opened, as well as more independent health-food retailers. This can increase competition for existing gyms, but it can also present opportunities for new ideas. So enterprises must be constantly aware of any changes in what consumers want.

Our increasing interest in exercise has led to an increase in gyms and personal trainers

Technological

Technology-related factors can impact the success of an enterprise.

Change

Technology helps businesses to work more efficiently, for example machinery can be faster at creating products in factories. However, this can also be very expensive for businesses to buy and keep replacing. Other businesses use technology for product innovations. For example, several companies now offer portable charging solutions for mobile phones, so that people can top up their battery when they are on the go. This taps into our ever-increasing reliance on our smartphones.

Automation

This includes the growing popularity of cashless purchases. For example to make travelling by London taxi easier, passengers can now pay for any journey using credit and debit cards, including contactless payments. This has required the purchase of new machines, meaning higher costs for the taxi operator.

Improved communications, the internet, internet marketing and social media

Technology can also improve the way businesses communicate with customers and each other. Most businesses nowadays have social media accounts to help customers get in touch and help the business to get key messages and promotions out to customers. This can increase sales and profits through increasing customer numbers.

Practise

Emma and Niva own a coffee shop called Gluttons. They specialise in serving Fairtrade coffee, hot chocolate and organic salads. They make and sell cakes and doughnuts and donate the profits to the local homeless charity.

They want to conduct a PESTEL analysis (see page 20). Explain two ethical influences that affect Gluttons.

Environmental factors and ethical trends

Environmental factors and ethical trends can also have a significant impact on the success of an enterprise.

Waste and recycling

The introduction of a law in 2015 making large shops charge 5p for a plastic bag has meant that some businesses have purchased paper bags to give to customers. These can be recycled and result in less waste going to landfill sites, but they are more costly to the business.

Carbon emissions and pollution

Businesses are aware of their CARBON EMISSIONS (harmful gases produced during transport or manufacturing) and pollution, and make a conscious effort to decrease this. This is done as it pleases customers, saves the business money and businesses must report their carbon usage to the government. If it is high, it gives a bad impression to customers, who might decide to buy from a business's competitors if their carbon usage is lower.

Impact on corporate social responsibility

The steps that a business takes to reduce the negative impacts that its activities have on communities and the environment is known as **CORPORATE SOCIAL RESPONSIBILITY**. An example of this is Sainsbury's changing the fridges in its stores to help reduce their carbon emissions. This has meant that companies are now investing more in their corporate social responsibility (CSR) projects so customers favour them over their competitors. If customers are happier with the CSR of a business, they are more likely to buy from it, so increasing the business's sales and profits.

Legal issues

Legal issues that can have an impact on the success of an enterprise include new laws and regulations: For example, the UK government increased the minimum wage (for workers aged over 25) from £7.20 to £7.50 from April 2017. This will influence businesses that employ people on the current minimum wage as it means their costs will go up and may mean they make less profit.

Techniques used to make decisions

To help them consider these factors, businesses use techniques such as **PESTEL ANALYSIS** (analysis used by a business to identify political, economic, social, technological, environmental and legal factors) and **SWOT ANALYSIS** (analysis used by a business to identify its strengths, weaknesses, opportunities and threats).

PESTEL analysis

A PESTEL analysis is used to better understand the operational environment, by breaking it down into the six categories of internal and external factors that have an impact on the success of an enterprise.

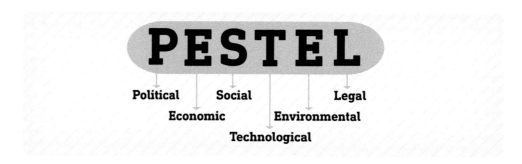

Figure 1.2: A PESTEL analysis will help you to understand the operational environment

SWOT analysis

A SWOT analysis is a technique that can be used to help a business classify its key strengths, weaknesses, opportunities and threats.

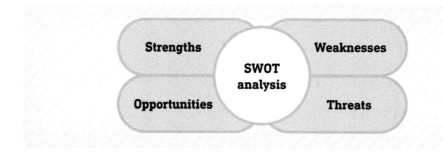

Figure 1.3: A SWOT analysis is a classic marketing tool that gives a quick overview of areas you need to focus on

Table 1.9: SWOT analysis

Internal factors	
Strengths	What the business does well For example: experience of staff, brand image, large range of products, customer service
Weaknesses	Areas that the business needs to improve For example: high levels of customers returning products or cancelling services, poor customer service, high staff turnover (how quickly employees leave the business)
External factors	
Opportunities	Developments that have happened in a market that the business might be able to take advantage of. However, because these are external factors the business has no control over them, so opportunities are also their competitors' opportunities. Businesses that successfully exploit opportunities gain an advantage For example: increased customer spending, changes in customers' tastes and preferences, newer technology
Threats	Uncontrollable events that may happen that could affect a business's success. Most businesses can foresee any potential threats and make plans for these For example: although the 2016 EU referendum result was a shock for most, businesses knew it was a possibility and could make some plans to limit its impact, despite uncertainty about how it will affect businesses in the future

Link it up

In Unit 2 (C3) you will practise using a PESTEL and SWOT analysis for your enterprise idea.

In Unit 4 (C1) you can practise using a SWOT analysis to reflect on your strengths and skills gaps.

Assessment practice   A04

Fred runs his own mobile tyre-fitting business, visiting customers at their home or place of work to fit new types to vans and cars. Another entrepreneur has just launched a similar business targeting the same geographical area.

Discuss whether a PESTEL or SWOT analysis would be more beneficial to Fred and consider how it could help his marketing planning. (6 marks)

Resources

Businesses must consider the resources that they have available to them when starting a new enterprise. These include the money needed to start and run the business, the tangible (physical) things needed to run the business, and the people and skills needed to run the business.

Table 1.10: Resources typically needed for a new enterprise

Physical resources	These include premises, materials, machinery and equipment. Businesses need to consider physical resources when assessing their likely success in the market. For example, if the rent on a shop increases, this increases costs and could affect profits. The business may then choose to move to a new location, but customers may not be willing to travel to the new location. Problems with the availability of suitable premises could affect customers and therefore sales and profits. Machinery, equipment or technology that the business needs to be able to compete in the market may be too expensive or need updating regularly. This creates an increase in costs for the business.
Human resources	The people that work for or with the business to help it be successful are known in business terminology as **HUMAN RESOURCES** (HR). Businesses need to consider their staff and ensure they have the correct expertise, experience and skills to help the business effectively. If there are high unemployment levels in the country, this could be good for businesses because it means there are more suitable people to choose from. However, if unemployment levels are low, there are fewer suitable people to choose from.

B2 Legal framework

Businesses are faced with several laws that impact on how they can behave. If businesses do not abide by these laws, they run the risk of heavy fines and negative media attention that can lead to a poor image and potential loss of customers.

Consumer protection

The principles of the Consumer Rights Act 2015 are:

- Products and digital content must be of satisfactory quality, fit for a particular purpose and match the description given.
- Services must be carried out with reasonable care and skill, within a reasonable time and for a reasonable price. The seller of services must also provide pre-contract information to the customer – information that they need about the service before they enter into the contract so they can make an informed decision.

Businesses must ensure that they abide by the above principles when selling products or services to customers and ensure that this is clear to customers. The act has different levels of action (known as tiered remedies) that can be taken if a business falls short of its duty (see Table 1.11). This means there are rights that a customer can exercise if a product or service is of an unsatisfactory quality.

Table 1.11: Tiered remedies

Tiers	Customers' rights under the Consumer Rights Act
Tier 1	Customers have a 30-day right to reject a product and obtain a refund. However, this does not apply to digital content, such as downloadable music, digital games and apps. If these are of unsatisfactory quality, customers can ask for them to be replaced or reduced in price.
Tier 2	After 30 days have passed, customers lose the right to simply return a product and get a refund without good reason. However, they do still have the right to get a product repaired or replaced. If the repair or replacement is still faulty, the customer can receive a full refund.
Tier 3	Tier 3 allows the customer to return a product and get a refund, or keep the product and have a price reduction. However, this tier is only available when the second tier has not brought about a satisfactory conclusion or is not possible due to the circumstances.

The customer is also protected if the seller decides to change the product that they are selling without telling them. This is called protection from unfair terms in consumer contracts.

All consumers are protected by the Consumer Rights Act 2015

Data protection

The Data Protection Act 1998 requires that any data collected from customers must be processed and used:

- fairly
- lawfully
- in line with customers' rights
- only for the purposes it was collected.

Businesses must ensure that the personal information they have on individuals is:

- up to date
- accurate
- not kept for longer than necessary
- not passed to anyone else without the individual's permission
- always kept safely and securely.

These principles may impact the way businesses keep information collected from market research, or information from loyalty cards and when customers sign up to company mailing lists.

What if...?

Martin runs a small carpentry business. He collects information about his customers so that he can contact and charge them for the work he completes. He has never thought to ask his customers whether their data can be used for other purposes. But one day Martin is contacted by a market research company that is looking to investigate people's buying habits around furniture. They offer to buy his customer list so that they can contact his customers as part of their research.

1 What should Martin consider before he makes his decision?

2 What could the consequences be for Martin if he does not operate within the correct legal framework?

3 Consider the outcome if businesses were allowed to sell personal data about their customers without their permission.

Consumer credit

The Consumer Credit Act 1974 requires that businesses that offer credit to customers (to pay for products or services in instalments over a period of time) clearly communicate the terms of the credit agreement, including the:

- amount of credit
- deposit paid
- number of payments
- total charge for credit
- cancellation and 'COOLING-OFF PERIOD' (the time within which the customer can change their mind and cancel the agreement).

These principles may impact the way businesses price their products or services and what credit agreements they offer to customers.

Health and safety

The Health and Safety at Work etc. Act 1974 means that businesses must ensure that they keep all of their employees, and anybody else who comes onto the business premises, safe.

> **CHECKLIST** | **HOW A BUSINESS ENSURES THE SAFETY OF EMPLOYEES AND VISITORS**
>
> ☐ Maintains a healthy and safe work environment
>
> ☐ Ensures safe working practices by specifying suitable procedures that employees must follow
>
> ☐ Identifies and assesses risks and hazards
>
> ☐ Provides suitable training, instruction and guidance for employees on manual handling (physically lifting heavy items) and use of equipment
>
> ☐ Provides employees with personal protective equipment (PPE)
>
> ☐ Follows the Control of Substances Hazardous to Health (COSHH) Regulations 2002
>
> ☐ Ensures products are labelled appropriately and accurately
>
> ☐ Reports and records any hazards, injuries, diseases and dangerous incidents

If businesses fail to follow any of the above principles, this is considered a breach of health and safety regulations, and the Health and Safety Executive (HSE) becomes involved. The role of the HSE is to enforce this act, give cautions to businesses that do not follow the act, and possibly even prosecute these businesses. Health and safety breaches and prosecutions increase businesses' costs and may damage their reputation. Employers may be held personally responsible for certain breaches. However, these principles ensure safe work environments for employees.

Equality

The Equality Act 2010 requires that businesses do not discriminate against employees and other people in the workplace because of certain characteristics (see Figure 1.4). It replaces previous anti-discrimination laws with a single act.

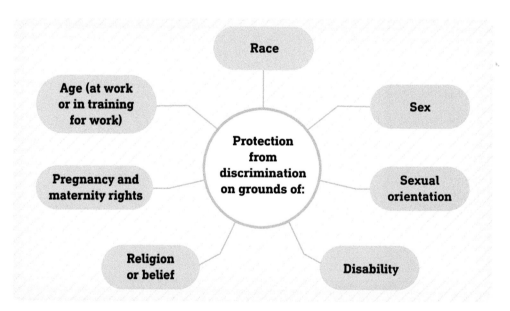

Figure 1.4: The Equality Act 2010

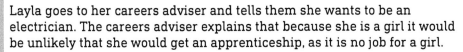

What if...?

Two friends are thinking about their future careers.

Layla goes to her careers adviser and tells them she wants to be an electrician. The careers adviser explains that because she is a girl it would be unlikely that she would get an apprenticeship, as it is no job for a girl.

Kanvil starts her apprenticeship at her local hairdressers. She ends the apprenticeship as her employer tells her that all staff have to wear their hair down to show the colours and styles to customers. Kanvil wears a hijab and is not prepared to do this as it is against her beliefs.

1 What laws are being broken?

2 What protected characteristics do both girls possess?

Skills and knowledge check

☐ What are the different resources that a business must consider for its success?

☐ What are the principles of the Consumer Rights Act and how does it impact businesses?

☐ What are the principles of the Data Protection Act and how does it impact businesses?

☐ What are the principles of the Consumer Credit Act and how does it impact businesses?

☐ What are the principles of the Health and Safety at Work Act and how does it impact businesses?

☐ What are the principles of the Equality Act and how does it impact businesses?

○ I can conduct a PESTEL analysis and a SWOT analysis for a business.

○ I understand the concept of corporate social responsibility.

C The contribution of enterprise to business success

C1 Enterprise and entrepreneurship

Entrepreneurs develop enterprises for many different reasons, but not all of them are successful.

Enterprise

Entrepreneurs are willing to spend time and risk money to make their ideas a reality; they also of course risk failing. There are several approaches for introducing a new product or service.

Identifying and creating a market need for a product or service

Some entrepreneurs are very good at convincing people they need a new product or service in their lives. Amazon's Echo had a successful advertising campaign convincing people of the need to have a voice-controlled device that plays music, reads the news and gives a weather forecast.

Identifying gaps in the market for existing products and services

Sometimes an existing product or service that has been successful in one market can also conquer a new market, if the right **PROMOTIONAL** techniques – those used by a business to promote and publicise their product – are used. For example, sports drinks and supplements, such as protein shakes and energy drinks, have always been popular among gym-goers and athletes. But some businesses have seen sales of these products grow by promoting them as part of a healthy lifestyle to non-athletes.

Creating products and services and identifying a market for them

When a product or service is created, entrepreneurs need to identify who in the market will buy it, and then, through promotion, try to persuade them to buy it. For example, the entrepreneur who developed iPrints (see page 12) identified the market as skiers and snowboarders who want to use their phone on the slopes and in the chair lifts.

Adapting techniques to increase business efficiency and improve profitability

Adapting existing products and services or creating new ways to increase business efficiency can bring enterprise opportunities. Some businesses may have been using the same products or services for a while, but may be interested in a new technique that has been developed to use the existing product or service that will help them to be more efficient and increase their profits. For example, a new plug-in may allow an existing software program to compare last year's costs and revenues with this year's more easily.

Adding value to differentiate the business from competitors

Giving added value to products or services can differentiate them from the competition. For example, some high-quality furniture shops will not only offer free delivery, but will assemble the furniture for you in your home.

Many businesses are interested in advances that will help them communicate more effectively

Developing new products and services

Solving problems with existing products can also be a good place to start. Digital boxes that allow viewers to record straight onto the hard drive, and even pause live TV programmes, were revolutionary when they were first introduced. Before that, people needed a separate video or DVD recorder to record from their TV.

Identifying new ways to increase business efficiency and profitability

Many business people use different types of communication to work more efficiently with their colleagues or with partner organisations. Google has developed innovative ways for businesses to interact using technology, saving time and money. Google Hangouts, Sheets, Drive and Gmail are some of the new technologies that Google has successfully introduced.

Entrepreneurship

Entrepreneurship is the entrepreneur's capacity and willingness to develop, organise and manage a business venture, along with its risks, to make a profit. This is often done through innovation. This is the development of new products/ services, methods or ideas by doing the actions listed above.

C2 Benefits and risks associated with enterprise and entrepreneurship

Enterprise, innovation and entrepreneurship have many benefits and risks.

Benefits

The benefits associated with enterprise, innovation and entrepreneurship can fall into a variety of categories.

Improvements to products, processes, services and customer experience

Entrepreneurs often find ways to improve products, services or user experience. For example, an innovation from the inventor James Dyson improved the simple electric fan. He created the Dyson Air Multiplier fan – customers are happy because it has no blades and is almost silent.

Business growth

When enterprises design successful products, this leads to more sales and increased profit levels. This allows businesses to have the money to grow, which creates more jobs, brings in more tax for the government and supports many other industries who supply them.

Development of new and niche markets

A **NICHE MARKET** is a small segment of the whole market that a product or service is focused on. The entrepreneur will create products or services that are highly specialised for enthusiasts of the product or service. For example, TV channels such as ESPN and Star Cricket are niche services that exist for sports enthusiasts.

Offering unique selling points

A **UNIQUE SELLING POINT (USP)** is the major feature of a product or service that makes it easy to sell or promote. For example, service providers often have USPs by offering extras, such as electricians completing jobs on Sundays. Dyson has developed its Dyson Airblade hand dryer, which it promotes as being the fastest, most hygienic dryer on the market.

Link it up

Go to Unit 2, learning aim A, to find more information on the risks and benefits of innovation and USPs.

Service providers, such as electricians, offer extras to gain customers, like working on Sundays

Improved recognition and reputation

By developing products, processes and services, entrepreneurs and their staff develop recognition and favourable reputations in the market. Because of this, customers often develop loyalty to the business and continue to buy its products or services.

Smarter working

When entrepreneurs and businesses use products and services that automate tasks or improve communication methods, they save time and money. For example, the use of Google Hangouts has meant that some business meetings are now done online, saving travel and meeting costs.

Risks

The risks associated with enterprise, innovation and entrepreneurship usually involve the business failing to address a problem or meet a requirement.

Failing to meet operational and commercial requirements

The products and services that entrepreneurs develop may not meet customers' needs, or the product itself may not work in the way that customers require. For example, some customers who bought the Samsung Galaxy Note 7 reported the batteries catching fire. The problem cost Samsung billions of pounds, as it had to recall all the phones that had been sold.

Failing to break even

New enterprises often struggle in the first year of trading. They have high costs in setting up the business and if they do not make enough sales, they will not make enough revenue to **BREAK EVEN** (the point at which the total cost of providing the product or service is equal to the income gained from selling it). Around half of UK start-ups fail in their first five years.

Cultural problems

The cultural problems that can bring risks to an enterprise include:

- *Resistance to change*: sometimes customers are not open to the changes that new products or processes can bring. They prefer the old or traditional way. This could mean that the product or process fails in a certain culture or generation or in a specific country, and will make it difficult for the enterprise to expand.
- *Unsupportive systems and processes*: new products or services have sometimes been developed, but the systems to support them are not in place. For example, older printers may not be compatible with new software upgrades, which can lead to customers not buying new generations of software.
- *Insufficient support from leadership and management*: entrepreneurs need to be supported by leadership and management within their business. If they do not have this, they may not be given the time and resources to innovate products.

Assessment practice //// **AO3**

Asif works for an IT company called Work IT. It specialises in wireless technology. Asif has an idea to create wireless household objects that can be operated using a smartphone.

Discuss the possible benefits and risks for Work IT if it decides to innovate. (6 marks)

C3 The skills required to be a successful entrepreneur

There are numerous skills and attributes that entrepreneurs need to be successful.

Skills

Starting your own business requires a mix of skills. Table 1.12 outlines the sort of abilities that successful entrepreneurs usually have.

Table 1.12: Entrepreneurial skills

Type of skill	Why it is needed
Practical/technical skills	Entrepreneurs need to be able to make the product or know a great deal about the service.
Interpersonal/ communication skills	Entrepreneurs need to be effective listeners, be able to question appropriately, have good and open body language and be assertive when necessary. For example, when dealing with customers, suppliers or banks to get funding.
Written communications skills	Entrepreneurs need to be able to write effectively. For example, letters and emails to customers/suppliers/banks. If their communication skills are poor, the correct message may not get across and the letter or email will look unprofessional.
Ability to deal with stress	Being an entrepreneur can be stressful. At the start of the business there may be little available cash, which can cause stress due to the need to borrow more money. The entrepreneur's ability to deal with these pressures is vital to the success of the enterprise.
Negotiation and problem-solving skills	• Entrepreneurs need to be able to negotiate with suppliers, for example, to get the best deals so that profit can be maximised on each product or service provided. • Entrepreneurs need to be able to solve problems. For example, problems may occur with the quality of the suppliers and solutions will need to be found to deal with these.
Time management skills	• Entrepreneurs need to be able to plan their time so as to avoid being overwhelmed with work and continue to meet customers' needs. • Entrepreneurs need to be able to set objectives that are SMART (specific, measurable, achievable, realistic and time-bound targets) and achieve these. • Entrepreneurs need to prioritise jobs to maximise efficiency and profit. • Entrepreneurs need to delegate jobs to other people where appropriate, to avoid an unmanageable workload.
Managing risk	Entrepreneurs need to know what risks affect the business and how to deal with them. For example, if after Christmas sales are slow, plans should be in place to overcome potential problems with cash flow. If risks are not managed, the business could get into financial difficulty.

Skills and knowledge check

☐ Explain some of the ways that entrepreneurs come up with new ideas.

☐ Explain the benefits of enterprise, innovation and entrepreneurship.

☐ Explain the risks of enterprise, innovation and entrepreneurship.

○ I can define entrepreneurship.

○ I can explain what skills are needed to be a successful entrepreneur.

Link it up

Go to Unit 4 to find more information on the skills needed to be an entrepreneur.

You will also learn to set SMART targets in Unit 4 (A2).

D Business enterprise ideas

D1 The suitability of a business idea

When entrepreneurs think of ideas, they then need to assess them to find out which one is most likely to be successful. The most amazing ideas may not be successful if the following factors are not considered.

Researching an idea for a product or service

Ideas can come from an entrepreneur's skills and abilities, or from identifying a gap in the market. When they have an idea, market research needs to be conducted. This enables businesses to find out what potential customers think of the idea.

Undertaking market research helps the entrepreneur to know whether the features of their product or service will provide benefits to potential customers. Based on the findings of the research, the entrepreneur will decide whether the idea is suitable for selection.

Resources required

Human resources

The people needed to make an idea work must be suitable. For example, does the entrepreneur have the correct skills to be able to bring the product or service to market? Do they have the time to be able to do this? If they do not have the required skills or time, do they know anybody who has? How much would it cost to get them involved?

Financial resources

The money needed to set up and run a business must also be sufficient, and the business's costs must not be excessive. For example, is there enough money to buy the resources to make a product or to buy a computer to create apps? The entrepreneur needs to be aware of the costs involved and keep these to a minimum.

Physical resources

The machinery, premises and materials needed to provide the product or service must be appropriate for the idea. The entrepreneur must consider where money can be saved. For example, would it be appropriate to work from home to provide a specific product or service, so saving costs, rather than rent a shop?

Likelihood of success or failure

Which idea is going to be most successful? The entrepreneur needs to consider:

a   access to customers
b   barriers to enterprise
c   will the product or service make a profit?
d   how much will each product or service make in profit and how could this be increased?

Access to customers and estimating demand

An entrepreneur will need to ask themselves who the potential customers for their product or service are. Are they easy to contact? Are there enough people out there who want to buy the product or service?

Providing a way for customers to access your product is important for its success

Barriers to enterprise

There are many factors that will make it difficult to set the business up. It is important to consider these and how they can be overcome.

*   *High start-up costs*: a large amount of money may be needed to start the business – such as buying expensive machinery – which needs to be borrowed.
*   *Cash flow issues*: you may need to spend a large amount of money to start making the product or providing the service and therefore not have a great deal of cash on which to live. It may be a long time before the business starts making enough money to pay back the initial costs.
*   *Licences and certification*: paperwork may be required for some types of business and can sometimes be expensive. This could include insurance certificates, registering with your local authority to make or sell food, or a licence either to sell alcohol or to sell food on the street.
*   *Skills and personal commitment required*: Does the entrepreneur have the right skills and passion to be able to make the product/service a success? How much time and energy is needed to make the product or run the service?

Plan and vision

If an idea is worth pursuing and investing in, an entrepreneur will need to consider how the product or service will be developed from an initial idea into a successful business.

*   *Possible customers*: who are the potential customers? What do they have in common? For example, their age, where they are based around the country or the world, what their interests and concerns are. Products or services can then be created to meet their needs.

- *Place and distribution*: where will the product or service be sold to best suit customers, and how will the entrepreneur supply it to them?
- *Strategy for dealing with competitors*: how is the product or service different from what competitors offer? This could be the actual product or service, where it is sold, the price or USP.
- *Ideas for financing*: where will the entrepreneur get money from to create the product or service?
- *Ideas for implementation*: how is the idea going to become a reality? How will this happen? How long will it take? How will the entrepreneur cope financially if the product or service does not start making a profit until the second year of the business? Does the entrepreneur have the necessary skills? If not, where are they going to get the training? Is this available? How much will it cost? Do they have the time?

Link it up

Go to Unit 2 (B1) and Unit 4, learning aim B, to find out more information on creative business ideas, developing a vision and pitching to potential investors.

Assessment practice   AO2

Explain why high start-up costs are a barrier to a new enterprise idea.
(4 marks)

D2 Sources of advice and finance

Entrepreneurs do not always have all the money and knowledge needed to set up their business. There are plenty of places they can get this:

Sources of finance

The money to start a business can come from a variety of sources. Many start-ups use a mixture of different types of funding.

Table 1.13: Finance

Type of funding	How a business can use this to its advantage
Owner's funds	Money that the entrepreneur has saved themselves. The more of this they have, the more likely banks and other people and organisations will be willing to lend to them.
Government funding	Money or tax breaks are provided by the government to help start-up businesses. There are usually criteria that you must meet to qualify.
Grants	Sums of money that do not need to be paid back. The Prince's Trust, for example, provide grants to support young people (aged 18–30) in setting up their own businesses.
Loans	Sums of money that are borrowed from a bank that are paid back with interest (a percentage of the amount borrowed on top of the original loan). A faultless business plan is needed, along with some of your own money to invest in the business.
Selling shares	If the business is a private limited company, the owner could sell shares in the business to family or friends in return for money that will be invested in the business.
Crowdfunding	Potential customers invest money in the new business, often just small amounts. Examples of schemes that facilitate this are Kickstarter and Crowdcube.
Business angels	The 'dragons' from the BBC show *Dragons' Den* are a type of business angel – they are individuals that invest money in start-up businesses in return for a stake in the business, and therefore also profit from it, if it is a success. They often bring contacts and experience to the business.
Venture capitalists	Venture capitalists invest in businesses, again for a stake in the company.
TRADE CREDIT	Trade credit is where you buy materials but do not need to pay for them straight away. This can be important for some businesses where they must buy a large amount of materials and can pay for them later to help their cash flow.
Hiring and leasing	Similar to renting. This is good for businesses that need to use expensive equipment because it means they do not have to buy it, which helps their cash flow.

Sources of advice

Getting advice from someone who has been successful in starting their own business can be invaluable to an entrepreneur who is starting up on their own for the first time.

Table 1.14: Advice

Type of organisation	How they can help
Support networks	Chambers of commerce, which can be found in many counties across the UK, are an example of a support network where a group of organisations support local businesses.
Trade associations	Organisations that offer support and guidance to their members who work in certain trades, for example electricians.
Professional bodies	Organisations that represent professionals, such as doctors and solicitors, and offer them support and advice.
Enterprise programmes	Young Enterprise and Tycoon in Schools are examples of enterprise programmes for young people who want to start their own business. They are given a nominal grant to see how much revenue they can generate, along with a mentor to help them.
Charities	The Prince's Trust is an example of a charity that helps young and disadvantaged people start up their own business. It offers training, mentoring, support and advice.
Government and voluntary organisations	Enterprise agencies are local bodies funded by the UK government, and other partners, to help entrepreneurs starting their own business. StartUp Britain is a national campaign started by entrepreneurs for entrepreneurs, offering advice and support.

D3 Finance and success of a business idea

Costs

A business has many costs to meet. Some of these are spent to get the business up and running and are called **START-UP COSTS**. Some costs must be paid throughout the business's life and are called **OPERATING (RUNNING) COSTS**.

If you were planning to open an ice-cream parlour, what would be your start-up and operating costs?

The owners of a new ice-cream parlour would need to find a way to cover their start-up costs until the business starts making money

Setting up an ice-cream parlour

Start-up costs	Operating (running) costs
• Furniture • Equipment (ice-cream machine and freezers) and installation • Advertising for the opening • Deposit for the shop	• Rent for the shop • Wages for staff • Electricity • Marketing in the local paper and leaflets to hand out • Business rates • Stock (cream, flavouring, chocolate, sprinkles, etc.)

Table 1.15: Start-up and operating costs

Remember: start-up costs are only encountered once – but operating costs are faced regularly for the lifetime of the business.

There are four types of operating costs, depending on whether a cost is directly linked to the number of products and services sold, or whether it remains the same regardless of how much is sold (see Table 1.16). In practice there is some crossover between these four terms, with fixed and indirect costs often bracketed together, and variable and direct costs frequently considered together as well.

Type of cost	Definition
Fixed	Costs that do not vary with the activity levels of making a product or providing service – for example if a business hires an ice cream van for the summer, the hire charge will remain the same regardless of how much ice cream is sold
Variable	Costs that are directly linked to products or services, such as raw materials – for example cup cake cases for a cake maker
Direct	A cost that can be linked to a specific product or service – for example a plumber buying a part for a customer's boiler
Indirect	Costs that are not directly linked to production, such as renting office space, heating bills and management salaries

Table 1.16: Examples of fixed, variable, direct and indirect costs

Total costs = fixed costs + variable costs per **UNIT** (each individual product that can be sold). The total costs are the total operating costs for the business. A slight complication is that variable costs are usually quoted per item, e.g. £1.50 per unit. So, to calculate total costs, you need to know how many units are being made and sold. To work out total costs:

* Multiply the variable costs per unit by the number made/sold.
* Then add the total to the fixed costs.

For example, if an ice-cream parlour sold 500 ice creams a week with £1.50 variable costs per ice cream and £200 of fixed costs, the *total costs* would be

$$\text{Variable costs} = £1.50 \times 500 = £750$$
$$\text{Fixed costs} = £200$$
$$\text{Total costs} = £750 + £200 = £950$$

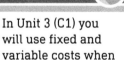

Link it up

In Unit 3 (C1) you will use fixed and variable costs when producing your financial plan.

Assessment practice /////// **A01**

Henry is setting up a gardening business and needs to purchase a lawnmower.

What type of cost will this be? (1 mark)

Select *one* option

☐ Variable cost   ☐ Start-up cost

☐ Direct cost   ☐ Indirect cost

Revenue

All businesses need revenue. This is the income a business receives from its sales.

For example, in an ice-cream parlour, the revenue source would be from the sale of ice creams. However, the business could also have other sources of revenue, such as rent received from a residential flat above the shop.

Calculate total revenue using this formula:

Total revenue = Number of sales × price per unit

For example, if the ice-cream parlour sells 500 ice creams at £2 each, the total revenue would be:

500 × £2.00 = £1 000

Profitability

Most businesses want to make a profit. Exceptions to this would be organisations that are run for social purposes and have a not-for-profit philosophy.

There are two types of profit: GROSS PROFIT and NET PROFIT.

1   Gross profit is calculated by subtracting the cost of sales from the sales revenue, i.e. the income from selling products minus how much they cost to make. The formula is:

Gross profit = Sales revenue – Cost of sales

For example, in our ice-cream parlour, the revenue was calculated as £1 000 for selling 500 ice creams at £2.00 per ice cream. If the variable cost of sales (cream, cones and sprinkles) came to £1.50 per ice cream, gross profit would be

£1 000 – (500 × £1.50) = £250

This seems like a great deal of profit, but do not be fooled. It takes more than cream, cones and sprinkles to make ice creams. What about the expenses the business will incur, such as freezers, staff wages, hire of an ice-cream machine, electricity and rent for the shop?

2   Net profit is the profit we have left after all these expenses have been paid:

Net profit = Gross profit – total expenses

For example, if our ice-cream parlour had expenses of £80 (rent, electricity, staff salaries, hire of ice-cream machine) then the net profit would be

£250 – £80 = £170

New businesses want to start making a profit as quickly as possible

Sometimes, businesses want to know how much profit they are making as a percentage of their whole income from sales. This is called the **PROFIT MARGIN**:

1 **GROSS PROFIT MARGIN** is the gross profit as a percentage of turnover
2 **NET PROFIT MARGIN** is the net profit as a percentage of turnover.

For example, in the ice-cream parlour:

The gross profit margin would be

$$\frac{£250}{£1\,000} \times 100 = 25\%$$

The net profit margin would be

$$\frac{£170}{£1\,000} \times 100 = 17\%$$

All businesses want a positive profit figure, because negative profit means that they are making a loss.

> **Link it up**
>
> In Unit 3 (C1) you will calculate profit levels when producing your financial plan.

Table 1.17: Gross and net profit

	Gross profit	Net profit
Positive figure	If gross profit is positive, the revenue is greater than the sales costs (the cost of raw materials needed for the production of the goods that are sold).	If net profit is positive, gross profit will also be positive, and the sales costs are within acceptable levels.
Negative figure	If gross profit is negative, then the business needs to either: • increase sales revenue, either by increasing the price per unit without decreasing sales, or by increasing the numbers of units sold • reduce sales costs (e.g. use cheaper materials, buy materials in bulk, get discounts from suppliers).	If net profit is negative, gross profit may be too low or costs too high. The business needs to either: • increase gross profit • reduce costs by assessing where savings can be made.

Capital

Current assets

CURRENT ASSETS are what the business owns on a day-to-day basis, including stock (raw materials and products), cash, and money owed to the business by others (debtors). Current assets can also be easily changed into money.

Current liabilities

CURRENT LIABILITIES are the amounts of money (liabilities) owed by the business to others that must be paid back within the next 12 months. The most common current liabilities are trade credit (money owed to other businesses for materials bought), bank overdrafts and dividends (payments to shareholders).

Working capital

WORKING CAPITAL (NET CURRENT ASSETS) is the money that the business has available, or that it expects to have soon, which enables it to pay for day-to-day costs, such as paying staff wages or buying raw materials. Working capital is calculated as

Working capital = Current assets – Current liabilities

If a business is running efficiently, it will have enough working capital to deal with day-to-day costs and any unforeseen problems.

> **Link it up**
>
> In Unit 3 (C1) you will look at other ways of monitoring cash flow.

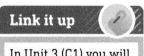

Liquidity

Ratios are used to calculate a business's LIQUIDITY (a business's ability to pay its debts) and PROFITABILITY (how much profit a business makes from sales of a product or service). Below are some of the formulas used in these calculations:

Liquid capital ratio (acid test)

The LIQUID CAPITAL RATIO or ACID TEST is a measure of a business's ability to pay off its current liabilities. With acid tests, stocks are not included in the calculation, because these may not always be sold within the current year. They are not as liquid as other current assets.

$$\text{Acid test ratio} = \frac{\text{Current assets} - \text{stock}}{\text{Current liabilities}}$$

For a healthy business, acid test ratios should be between 0.8 and 1.0.

Current ratio

The CURRENT RATIO is a measure of how easily a business can pay off its current liabilities from its current assets, in other words how easily it can pay its short-term debts.

$$\text{Current ratio} = \frac{\text{Current assets}}{\text{Current liabilities}}$$

For a healthy business, current ratios should be between 1.5 and 2.0. To get the required information, you will need to see the business's BALANCE SHEET (statement of financial position).

Importance of liquidity

The more liquid an asset, the more quickly it can be turned into cash. A lack of liquidity for a business can cause financial problems to the business. For example, If the business needs money quickly to pay off suppliers, but it does not have any assets that can be easily changed into cash, such as products or stock, the business may eventually become insolvent.

Break even

Break-even analysis

It is important for a business to know when it will make a profit from a business activity. It finds this out by calculating the amount of sales it needs to cover its costs.

When a business breaks even, it is making no profit and no loss. This means that the total costs of providing the products or services are the same as the income that is coming in from selling them.

The BREAK-EVEN POINT is where

Total costs = Total revenue

For example, suppose a jeans manufacturer were to produce 40 pairs of jeans and the total cost of making these was £4000. If 40 pairs of jeans were sold for £100 each, the total revenue would be £4000.

£4000 – £4000 = £0, so the jeans manufacturer would make no profit, but nor would it make a loss, and therefore the business would break even.

Risks of not completing a break-even analysis

If a start-up business does not complete its break-even analysis:

- it will not know how long it will take the business to make a profit
- it will not know if the business is viable and how risky it is to start up.

A break-even analysis is important because it lets businesses see how any changes in the costs of their raw materials will affect their ability to make a profit. A break-even analysis is also important to see how any fall in sales could affect the business's profitability.

Limitations of a break-even analysis

Although a break-even analysis is a useful tool, it has limitations.

- Variable costs do not always stay the same, so this makes calculation more difficult, and the break-even point could be constantly changing.
- Businesses often have more than one product or service on sale at any one time, so it can become complicated to calculate this for multiple products.
- Break-even analysis assumes that everything that is produced is sold. But this is not always true – some stock may never be sold, particularly if it involves perishable goods.
- For the above reasons, break-even calculations should be used as a planning aid rather than a decision-making aid.

Break-even chart

A break-even chart can be constructed to find the break-even point.

For example, suppose the selling price per pair of jeans is £100, the variable costs are £40 per pair of jeans and the fixed costs are £2 400.

Table 1.18: Example of a break-even chart

Number of pairs of jeans sold	Total revenue: quantity x price (£)	Fixed costs (£)	Total variable costs: quantity x variable costs (£)	Total fixed costs + Variable costs (£)
0	0	2 400	0	2 400
20	2 000	2 400	800	3 200
40	4 000	2 400	1 600	4 000
60	6 000	2 400	2 400	4 800

If this jeans manufacturer estimated its sales at just 40 pairs of jeans, it would not risk production, because if just one fewer pair of jeans was sold, they would make a loss.

Margin of safety

The **MARGIN OF SAFETY** is the reduction in sales that can occur before the break-even point of a business is reached.

For example, for our jeans manufacturer, if the break-even point is 40 pairs of jeans, and the manufacturer estimates sales of 50 pairs of jeans, the margin of safety is 10 pairs of jeans, i.e. level of output (50) minus the break-even point (40). It is useful for the manufacturer to know that sales could fall by 10 pairs of jeans before it made a loss.

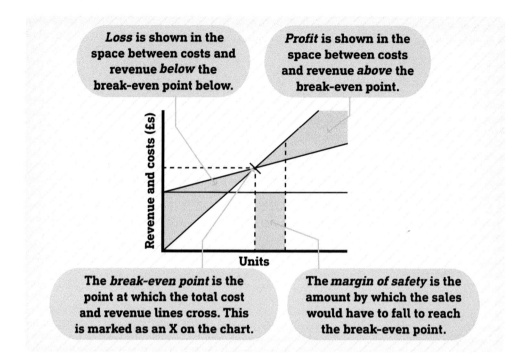

Loss is shown in the space between costs and revenue *below* the break-even point below.

Profit is shown in the space between costs and revenue *above* the break-even point.

The **break-even point** is the point at which the total cost and revenue lines cross. This is marked as an X on the chart.

The **margin of safety** is the amount by which the sales would have to fall to reach the break-even point.

Figure 1.5: When calculated, the break-even point can be shown on a graph

Calculating break-even by formula

You can also find the break-even point using the formula

$$\text{Break-even} = \frac{\text{Fixed costs}}{(\text{Selling price} - \text{Variable costs})}$$

So, for the jeans manufacturer, selling price – variable costs = £100 – £40 = £60

The fixed costs are £2 400, so the number of pairs of jeans that needs to be sold to break even is

$$\frac{£2\,400}{£60} = 40 \text{ pairs of jeans}$$

Remember: you could be asked to re-arrange the break-even formula in the assessment. For example, you could be asked to calculate the selling price if you were given the fixed costs and variable costs.

Effect on break-even point if sales or costs change

The break-even point changes if sales or costs change. For example, if the jeans manufacturer has to pay more for materials to make the jeans, its costs will increase. It will either have to increase the selling price (which could mean it sells fewer) or earn less money on each pair of jeans sold. This means it will need to sell more to break even.

Table 1.19: Influences on break-even point

Type of change	Effect of change on break-even point
Increase in sales	The margin of safety increases.
Decrease in sales	The margin of safety decreases. If sales fall below the break-even level, the business could make a loss.
Increase in costs	The number of sales required to break even increases, so the profit level falls or even becomes a loss.
Decrease in costs	The break-even point is lower, so the business makes more profit.
Increase in selling price	The number of sales required decreases. If sales stay the same, profit increases.
Decrease in selling price	The number of sales required to break-even increases.

Increased sales and decreased costs are good for a business. However, if sales fall or costs increase, then action must be taken before the business makes a loss. If price of the material to make the jeans increases, the business could look at a cheaper substitute or try to get the same material cheaper from another supplier.

Link it up

For an example of a cash-flow forecast, look at Unit 3 (C1).

Cash-flow forecasting

A **CASH-FLOW FORECAST** is a record of all the cash that has flowed into the business (**INFLOWS**) and the cash that has flowed out of the business (**OUTFLOWS**) in a given time period.

Purpose, importance and benefits

The purpose of cash-flow forecasting is to enable businesses to predict the inflows and the outflows. The cash-flow forecast is important because:

- it is often looked at by lenders to make sure that it would not be too risky to invest in that business
- from it, the business owners will hope to foresee any times when there will be possible cash-flow problems, and act to avoid them.

Impact of timings of inflows and outflows

Inflows and outflows and their timings can have an impact on a business. For example, if there is not enough cash one month, the business can either delay paying creditors or arrange for an overdraft.

Risks of not completing a cash-flow forecast

The risks associated with not completing a cash-flow forecast are:

- Lenders might decide not to invest in the business.
- If the business does not have sufficient cash to cover its day-to-day costs, it will have cash-flow problems.

Identifying cash-flow problems

A cash-flow problem may happen because customers buy products on credit. This means that sales and profits have been made, but the cash has not yet been received by the business.

Another reason might be that the business has used a large amount of cash to buy stock, but it has not yet been able to sell these items. Until the business sells its stock, it will not receive any cash.

If a business forecasts a cash-flow problem, it can arrange an overdraft or try to buy more of its supplies using credit. It could also try to make sure that most of its customers pay for their purchases straight away.

Remember: Negative numbers in cash flow are presented in brackets, e.g. (£1 000) means –£1 000.

Even well-established businesses can have cash flow problems if they have to make large payments to their suppliers before their customers have paid them

Assessment practice

Natasha owns a cinema. She predicts what is going to happen over the next 6 months:

Expected receipts are:

Table 1.20: Expected receipts

July	August	September	October	November	December
£84 000	£68 000	£80 000	£88 000	£96 000	£120 000

She also predicts the following payments:

Table 1.21: Payments

	July	August	September	October	November	December
Purchase of confectionery	£14 000	£11 000	£13 000	£15 000	£16 000	£20 000
New release films	£6 000	£6 000	£6 000	£6 000	£8 000	£8 000
Staff wages	£11 000	£11 000	£11 000	£11 000	£12 000	£13 000
Utilities	£2 000	£2 000	£2 000	£2 000	£3 000	£3 000
Advertising	£15 000	£15 000	£15 000	£30 000	£30 000	£25 000
Loan repayments	£20 000	£20 000	£20 000	£20 000	£20 000	£20 000
Miscellaneous	£3 000	£3 000	£4 000	£3 000	£5 000	£4 000

The closing balance of cash in June is predicted to be (£17 000).

1 Produce a cash-flow forecast for Natasha. (6 marks)

2 Explain why sales receipts might be higher in the winter months. (1 mark)

3 In which months does the cinema have a cash-flow issue? (1 mark)

4 Suggest two ways in which the cinema could solve its cash-flow problems in these months. (2 marks)

Skills and knowledge check

- ☐ Evaluate costs, revenue, profitability, capital and liquidity.
- ☐ Complete a break-even analysis using the formula and graph.
- ☐ Explain the limitations of break-even analysis and the risks if not completed.
- ☐ Explain the effect on the break-even point if sales or costs change, and the impact of these changes.
- ☐ Explain the purpose and importance of cash-flow forecasting.
- ☐ Explain the benefits and risks of not completing a cash flow.

- ◯ I can assess the suitability of a business idea.
- ◯ I can explain the sources of finance and advice.
- ◯ I can complete a cash-flow forecast from given information and interpret this, identifying problems.

WORK FOCUS

HANDS ON

There are some important technical and professional skills and competencies that you will need to practise that relate to this unit and your role as a potential entrepreneur. Developing and practising these will help you make a good impression in work experience placements as well as gain employment in the future.

Ideas for products and services: good or bad?

- Consider this list of innovative products. Rate the ideas in terms of their viability; 1 being utterly ridiculous and 5 being innovation of the year.

- Comment on whether you think they are a good idea or bad and explain they are or are not viable to create.

  ○ Women's shoes with a detachable heel – for busy working women who want to go straight from the office wearing flat shoes to a restaurant wearing heels.

  ○ iPad holder for a potty – children could watch the iPad hands free during their toilet training.

  ○ Bread Gloves – gloves that are made of bread so you could make anything into an immediate sandwich!

  ○ PC keyboard with docking space for your smart phone to sit in.

  ○ Detachable handle you can attach to a can so you can drink with ease.

Researching an idea for a product or service

- As a budding entrepreneur, consider any products or services you could develop. Think about what you could use to make your daily life easier, research on the internet, ask family and friends, consider what skills you already possess. Create a digital 'thought board' of these ideas. Consider the strengths, weaknesses, opportunities and threats for each idea.

- You could now consider the viability of each of these ideas. Could you afford to create them/set them up? Do you have the skills/ knowledge? How do you know people will want to purchase your product/service?

Giving reasons for selection

- Select 2 or 3 of your ideas. Create a video where you talk to the camera, explaining why you believe these are the best ideas.

Ready for work?

Imagine you are ready to set up your own enterprise. You are looking to create and sell an app that notifies people about the upcoming birthdays of their family and friends. You would like it to track and remind users about the last few gifts they gave to people.

- Would you be ready to be an entrepreneur?
- Would you have the skills, knowledge and confidence to set up an enterprise offering this service?

- What skills/knowledge gaps would you have? How could you ensure that you gained the necessary skills/knowledge?

- How would your communication skills be used to set up this enterprise?

- How would your time management skills be used to set up this enterprise?

- How would your problem-solving skills be used to set up this enterprise?

- Create a checklist of dos and don'ts to bear in mind if you were to set up this enterprise.

Getting ready for assessment

This section has been written to help you to do your best when you take the external test. Read through it carefully, and ask your tutor if there is anything you are not sure about.

About the test

This unit is assessed using an onscreen test, set and marked by Pearson. The test will be taken under controlled examination conditions. There will be three types of question: short answer (multiple choice), calculation questions and longer answer questions.

- An onscreen notepad will be provided for you to make notes during the test. These notes will not be marked.

- An onscreen calculator will be provided for questions that need calculation.

- An accessibility panel will be provided on every screen. This will allow you to zoom in or out and apply different colours.

- The number of marks for each question will be shown in brackets. Use this as a guide to how much time you should spend on each question.

Understanding the questions

Most of the questions will contain 'command words'. Understanding what these words mean will help you understand what the question is asking you to do.

Table 1.22: Command words and definitions

Command word	Definition – what it is asking you to do
Analyse	Examine in detail the meaning or essential features of a topic or situation. Break it down into the different parts and say how they are related. Explain how each part contributes to the topic or situation.
Assess	Consider a variety of factors that apply to a specific situation, or identify those that are most important or relevant in order to arrive at a conclusion.
Calculate	Use maths to determine the answer.
Complete	Provide the items needed to make a list.
Discuss	Consider different aspects of the topic, how they relate to each other and how important they are.
Evaluate	Use different information to consider aspects such as strengths and weaknesses, advantages or disadvantages, alternative actions, and relevance or significance, and come to a conclusion.
Explain	Show you understand the subject. Give reasons to support an opinion, view or argument, with clear details.
Give	Provide examples, justifications and/or reasons in context.
Identify	Indicate the main features or purpose of something.
Match	Choose an item that corresponds to another, to make a similar or complementary pair.
Name	Give the written term that the object of the question is identified by.
Outline	Give a general description showing the essential features of something, but not the detail.
State	Give a definition or example.

Sample questions and answers

Question 1

This question is testing your ability to demonstrate understanding and application of enterprise principles relating to the business environment. Start by making a relevant point and expand on it by using two or three steps in a logical line of argument. Remember to use linking words, such as 'therefore', 'so that' and 'because'. Avoid moving onto new points in your argument until you have fully developed each one.

Fleur is a successful personal trainer. She is a sole trader who currently works from home where she has converted her front room into a gym. Her main business is in training women on a one-to-one basis. She would like to rent a larger gym space on the high street. This could be used as an office, a gym and a changing room with a shower. Fleur thinks that locating to the new premises would increase her profits.

Explain why Fleur should move her personal training business to the high street premises. (4 marks)

Student answer

If she moved to the new premises she could use the gym to expand into other areas of personal training, for example training men, or group/couple training, not just individual women. This location would increase the number of people who walk past her shop and raise her profile in the area. This will hopefully make the business more profitable and cover the costs of moving.

Verdict

This answer would get high marks, as there are several steps that have been given in a logical argument:

1. if she moved she could expand into other areas of personal training
2. location will increase the number of people walking past her shop
3. which will raise her profile
4. and make the business more profitable and cover the costs of moving.

Question 2

Eydi and Yula enjoy baking. They have created a chocolate cake that also contains chilli. Their family and friends loved their chilli chocolate cake so much that Eydi and Yula decided to start their own business making cakes containing chilli. They went to their local market and started selling.

Identify Eydi and Yula's main unique selling point (USP). (1 mark)

Student answer

Chilli in cakes

Verdict

1 Providing the correct answer is all that is needed for a 1-mark question. Chilli is not usually found in cakes and sweet goods and is therefore what makes them stand out from their competitors and could be a reason customers buy from them.

2 You will be asked a variety of identify or multiple choice answers. The number of answers you need to select or give will be indicated by the number of marks for the question.

Question 3

Analyse how demographic trends impact the success of a business. (6 marks)

Student answer

1 Demographic trends include population trends, for example whether the population is ageing or not. An ageing population demands different products and services than a young population and so if a business is to succeed it must produce something to suit older people in an ageing population. However, it is costly to keep on researching and producing products and services based on demographics as these can change all of the time. In order to be successful, businesses would also need to consider the type of customer to target within the ageing population and create products that meet their needs effectively.

2 Demographic trends will affect the demand for different products and services and so if a business is to succeed it must be located appropriately and products/services need to be priced appropriately.

Verdict

This question is testing your ability to evaluate business data and make informed judgements. Remember to present two arguments from different viewpoints, such as one advantage and one disadvantage or one argument for and one argument against.

1 This answer uses the command word 'analyse', so you need to make a logical argument made up of several steps and to show informed judgements of advantages/disadvantages and possible outcomes:

- demographics include population trends

- which include whether the population is ageing or not

- an ageing population demands different products and services to a young population and so if a business is to succeed it must produce something to suit older people in an ageing population

- however, it is costly to keep researching and producing products and services based on demographics as these can change all of the time

- businesses would also need to consider the type of customer to target within this older population and create products that meet their needs effectively.

2 This answer is less effective because it does not first identify what is meant by demographic trends and what aspect of these trends will affect the demand. A fuller answer would be:

- demographic trends include population trends

- which includes whether the population is ageing or not

- both will affect the demand for different products and services

- and so if a business is to succeed it must be located appropriately and products/services need to be priced appropriately.

2 Researching a Concept for a New or Revised Product or Service

Have you ever dreamed of setting up your own business or developing an idea for a new product or service? What type of enterprise skills do you think you need to be successful? How could you develop these skills to make your enterprise idea a success?

In this unit you will learn how people use enterprise skills to develop new businesses or new ideas within a business. You will gain an understanding of the types of skills they have used and use a range of techniques to develop your own creativity to develop enterprise ideas.

How will I be assessed?

Because this unit is assessed by your school or college, you will work with your tutors and entrepreneurs to produce a portfolio of evidence that covers the assessment criteria outlined below. You will investigate a case study of a start-up business and a case study of an enterprise activity within an existing business. You will use this to explain, analyse and evaluate the features that make enterprise ideas successful, and to identify the benefits and risks of enterprise.

You will need to use a range of creativity techniques to develop enterprise ideas. You will need to think about each of your ideas and select a good enterprise idea, giving reasons why you have rejected the other ideas. You will need to identify a target market and then use a range of high-quality market research techniques to evaluate your enterprise idea.

Assessment criteria

Pass	Merit	Distinction
Learning aim A: Investigate how enterprise skills contribute to business success		
A.P1 Explain the features of successful enterprise ideas and how they were generated.	**A.M1** Analyse how enterprise ideas have been developed and implemented.	**A.D1** Evaluate the features that make enterprise ideas successful.
A.P2 Identify the benefits and risks of enterprise.		
Learning aim B: Generate enterprise ideas using creativity techniques		
B.P3 Develop a new credible enterprise idea.	**BC.M2** Refine a selected enterprise idea using market research methods appropriate for the target market.	**BC.D2** Assess a selected enterprise idea using high-quality market research methods tailored to the target market.
B.P4 Give reasons why ideas should be discounted.		
Learning aim C: Investigate market research for a selected enterprise idea.		
C.P5 Use a range of market research methods to investigate an enterprise idea.		

A Investigate how enterprise skills contribute to business success

Within this unit you will need to develop an **ENTERPRISE IDEA**.

A1 Enterprise ideas

Types of enterprise idea include the following.

New products or services

A business or an entrepreneur develops a completely new product or service for sale. For example, Shaun Pulfrey's new enterprise idea for a product called the Tangle Teezer was turned down by investors on the BBC show *Dragons' Den*. But he went on to develop it to combine the best parts of a comb and a brush, and signed a deal with the pharmacy chain Boots to sell it.

Revising existing products or services

Sometimes a business may choose to adapt the design, construction or function of a product or service slightly. For example, women's fashion retailer Topshop launched the men's clothing store Topman.

Redeveloping existing products or services

When a product or service starts to become less popular, the entrepreneur may choose to redevelop the product or service to improve it. This usually involves launching a new version of the product or service entirely, rather than just adapting it. For example, Ford frequently redevelops its range of cars, including launching new models of the Mondeo and the Fiesta.

Practise

1. Make a list of all the new products or services you can think of in an industry or market.

2. Select a product or service already being sold. Revise the product, slightly changing its design, construction or function. This might also include adapting the **MARKETING MIX** for the product or service. The marketing mix is the combination of product, price, place and promotion. This is also called the **FOUR PS**.

3. Using the same product or service, or a different one, redevelop the product or service to improve it. How could you make it better and more popular?

Link it up

The marketing mix is covered later in this unit. Look at C1 when you do this Practise activity.

The product life cycle

Every product or service has a **PRODUCT LIFE CYCLE**. During this, a product or service will go through the following stages.

Figure 2.1: The life cycle of a product shows how it can be expected to perform over time

Development stage

This is the first stage any product or service goes through. It is where enterprise ideas are generated. When the enterprise idea has been created, **MARKET RESEARCH** needs to be carried out to ensure that the idea is workable and will be successful. Market research involves gathering information on potential customers, on what they are likely to be able to pay for the product or service, and on potential competitors. Your enterprise idea is currently in this stage, and your work throughout this unit will allow you to experience the development stage in the product life cycle.

Introduction stage

This is the stage where the enterprise idea is introduced to the market and starts to be sold. A lot of time and money will go into ensuring that this stage is successful in informing customers about the product or service and persuading them to buy it.

Growth stage

When a product or service is successful, it will grow in popularity and sales will increase. It is important at this stage that the business constantly reminds customers of the benefits of the product or service, to ensure that people keep buying it.

Maturity stage

The most successful products or services in a market will be in the maturity stage of the product life cycle. In this stage, the reputation of the product or service is at its strongest, and sales are at their maximum levels. Businesses aim to keep their products in the maturity stage of the product life cycle for as long as possible by using strategies to revise and redevelop an existing product or service. They will also use the marketing mix to encourage customers to keep buying them.

Decline stage

Inevitably, some products or services go out of fashion, and sales start to fall. Businesses will work hard in these circumstances, using strategies to revise and redevelop the product or service, and the marketing mix to stop the decline in sales. Often, during this stage, new competitors have entered the market with more attractive products or services. If businesses are not successful in preventing the fall in sales, the product or service will enter the decline stage of the product life cycle, and they will lose **MARKET SHARE**. Market share is the proportion of the market dominated or controlled by a business. The product or service will probably be removed from the market, and replaced with a new enterprise idea or a redeveloped product or service.

Link it up

Market research is covered later in this unit. Look at learning aim C to find out more.

In Unit 4 (B1), when you present your business plan to an audience, you will also need to provide the reasons behind your enterprise idea and how you can tell it will be successful.

What if...?

Danny and Samil have been running their market stall selling CDs and DVDs since 2001. In recent years they have found that demand for their products has fallen and they are now struggling to make a living from the market stall. They have organised a meeting with a local business adviser to consider the options available.

1 How could Danny and Samil use the product life cycle to help them consider what is going wrong with their business?

2 What revision and development strategies could they introduce to help increase the number of customers visiting their market stall?

Looking critically at enterprise ideas

When preparing for your assessment in this unit, you will need to think about the enterprise idea you are developing. You will look at the product life cycle of other products or services in the market to ensure that your enterprise idea can compete with them and be successful. You will also need to think about when you might need to revise and redevelop products or services at different stages of the product life cycle.

Looking at real-world examples of businesses, the life cycles of their products and their markets will help you develop your enterprise idea.

For example, Apple introduced the iPhone in 2007. The product grew in popularity and the number of sales, reaching the maturity stage where it became a market leader in the smartphone industry. Since then, other competitors such as Samsung, HTC and Sony have introduced their own versions. In response, Apple has had to redevelop its iPhone to maintain its market share and maximise sales. These revision and redevelopment strategies have helped Apple's iPhone to stay in the maturity stage for a long time. In the future, Apple may find that its iPhone becomes less popular and so it may enter the decline stage.

Practise

Select a market or industry of your choice.

1 Research the main products and services available in the market or industry you have chosen.

2 Plot each of the products and services onto a product life cycle diagram such as the one on page 51 of this unit (Figure 2.1).

3 Identify at what point or points in the product life cycle the products or services may have been revised or redeveloped.

A2 Features of successful enterprise ideas

While there is no secret formula for creating successful enterprise ideas, many start-ups that have stood the test of time have certain features in common (see Figure 2.2).

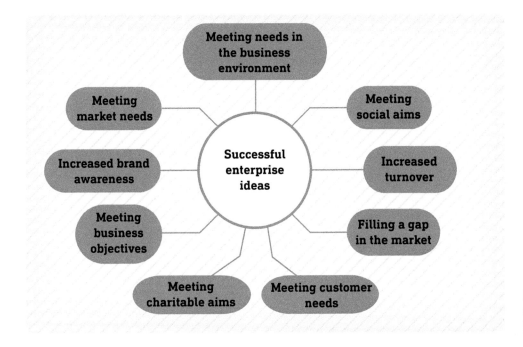

Figure 2.2: Successful enterprise ideas will have at least some of these features

When creating an enterprise idea, it is important to consider these features and look at how other businesses have used them to ensure that their products and services are successful.

Meeting market needs

For an enterprise idea to be successful, it is important to identify the needs of the market and any gaps in the market, and ensure that the enterprise idea meets these needs.

Meeting needs in the business environment

The **BUSINESS ENVIRONMENT** (the internal and external factors that influence a business) is always changing. For example, new competitors are frequently entering and leaving the market, new laws are often being introduced and price levels are constantly changing. It is important for businesses to identify these changes and adapt the enterprise idea to help them respond to the changes.

Increased turnover

TURNOVER is the **REVENUE**, or income, generated from making sales. It is calculated by:

Number of sales × Price of the product

A business that increases its turnover will have a greater chance of making more **PROFIT**, which is the money that a business makes once it has covered all its costs. Increased turnover will also increase market share and, as sales grow, the reputation of the idea will also get more exposure, making it more successful.

Increased brand awareness

To make a product or service successful, it is vital to create a strong **BRAND** image. A brand is a trademark or distinctive name identifying a product or service. The term is often applied to a product or service that stands out in the market. It will have a logo that is easily identifiable and strong **BRAND VALUES** (qualities that customers associate with the product or service). Brand awareness can be created by using the marketing mix to communicate to customers the benefits of the product or service to persuade them to buy it. Creating a **UNIQUE SELLING POINT (USP)** is also important in creating brand awareness. The USP is the factor, or factors, that make the product or service different to those of competitors, to make it stand out in the market. If the USP is created successfully, customers will recognise the product or service and keep buying it instead of others on the market.

Meeting business objectives

Every business sets its own objectives. These are targets that the business aims to achieve. Examples include maximising profit and maximising sales. Meeting these objectives will help the business judge how successful it is and allow it to set further objectives for the future.

Meeting customer needs

When creating an enterprise idea, it is important to identify the needs of customers. Businesses will carry out market research to gather information on their customers and their needs. These needs could be about what the customers want the product or service to do or how much they want to pay for it, but it could also include things such as good customer service. Making sure that customer needs are met ensures that people will buy the product or service again in the future. They will also spread awareness of it among their friends, family and colleagues, helping it to be more successful.

Filling a gap in the market

When the needs of the market have been identified, it is important to identify any gap in the market and design the enterprise idea so that it fills this gap. This will help to make your product or service stand out from others on the market and help to achieve brand awareness. For example, Rob Law invented the Trunki sit-on suitcase after identifying there was a gap in the market for an attractive, hard-wearing suitcase that appealed to children. If you do not fill a gap in the market, but merely offer something similar to that of your competitors, it will be difficult to encourage people to buy your product or service instead of others, and so your enterprise idea will not be successful.

Meeting social aims

All businesses need to think about the impact their actions have on others. Many businesses now include social aims in their business objectives. These include ensuring that the business does not damage the environment and that it uses suppliers that do not exploit their workers. Social aims help the business to create a positive impression on potential customers and avoid negative publicity. This will then create more sales and so make the enterprise idea more successful. For example, Innocent promotes sustainability as one of the key objectives for its smoothies, using sustainable materials in its products to reduce waste and encourage recycling.

Meeting charitable aims

In a similar way to setting social aims, businesses will also sometimes set charitable aims to ensure that they are 'giving back' to society and so creating a positive image of themselves to the public. Often they will identify one charity each year and carry out fundraising activities for it throughout the year. This helps to make the business's enterprise idea more successful because people may be more likely to buy it if they think that this will help a charity.

Link it up

In Unit 3, learning aim A, you will look in more detail at the concept of brand awareness.

In Unit 1, learning aim B, you will have already examined the external environment and its impact on the development and implementation of enterprise ideas.

Practise

Think about your list of enterprise ideas you generated earlier in this unit. For each idea, identify whether it has the features of successful enterprise ideas listed above.

A3 Types of enterprise

There are two types of enterprise: **ENTREPRENEURSHIP** and **INTRAPRENEURSHIP**.

Entrepreneurship

Entrepreneurship involves setting up a new business start-up. For example, Levi Roots created his enterprise idea, Reggae Reggae sauce, while setting up his business. His business is now very successful, after appearing on the BBC TV programme *Dragons' Den* and achieving financial support from established business owner Peter Jones.

Intrapreneurship

Intrapreneurship involves a new idea or revised idea within an existing business. Richard Branson has been very successful in using intrapreneurs and intrapreneurship programmes. Over a number of years his company Virgin has developed a number of new enterprise ideas such as airlines, trains, media companies. He is famous for creating successful enterprise ideas and then selling the companies on before moving on to another idea.

Link it up

You may want to look at how Levi Roots communicated his idea to an audience to help you think about how you will **PITCH** (formally present) your own idea in Unit 4, learning aim B.

Businesses owned by the Virgin Group include everything from rail services to gyms. Can you think of any other examples of successful intrapreneurs?

Your work in this unit involves researching and developing a new enterprise idea for a product or service. So, you could either choose entrepreneurship, by setting up a new business start-up, or choose intrapreneurship by creating a new idea, or revised idea, within an existing business.

Practise

Select a well-known business of your choice. Practise being an intrapreneur by creating a list of ideas for new products and services that it could sell under the name of its business.

A4 Enterprise skills

When generating an enterprise idea for a new product or service, the entrepreneur, or intrapreneur, will need a range of enterprise skills to help them to be successful in this role. During this unit you will need to develop and then practise these skills.

There are three main enterprise skills you will need to develop:
1 identifying gaps in the market
2 identifying problems
3 developing solutions to problems.

Practise

Do you have what it takes to be a successful entrepreneur? List the necessary skills, abilities and knowledge you think you already have and those you think you will need to acquire or improve on.

Link it up

In learning aim C, later in this unit, you will find more information on market research techniques.

Identifying gaps in the market

You will need to be able to identify any gap in the market so that you can develop your product or service to fill it. This will involve undertaking some market research about the local and national market.

The Cereal Killer Café filled a gap in the market after its owners discovered there were no other cafés focusing purely on breakfast cereal

Practise

Think about the enterprise ideas you developed earlier in this unit. Research your local area, identifying businesses that offer a similar product or service.

1 Where is there a gap in the market?

2 What are the other businesses failing to offer?

3 How would you develop your product or service so that it is different and fills this gap?

Link it up

You learned about doing a SWOT analysis in Unit 1. It is covered in more detail in learning aim B of this unit. Look at that section to help you here.

Identifying problems

You will need to identify any problems with your enterprise idea. You could use a **SWOT ANALYSIS** to help you think about the strengths, weaknesses, opportunities and threats relating to your enterprise idea.

Developing solutions to problems

If you have identified any problems with your enterprise idea, you will need to provide solutions to them and refine your enterprise idea based on those solutions.

Practise

Think about the enterprise ideas you developed earlier in this unit.

1 Produce a SWOT analysis on the enterprise idea.

2 When you have identified the weaknesses and threats of the idea, suggest possible solutions to these problems.

3 Based on the problems and solutions identified, refine your enterprise idea to ensure that it will be successful.

A5 The risks of lack of enterprise

Businesses that fail to develop enterprising ideas face risks on several fronts. These risks could have negative consequences for the long-term well-being of the business.

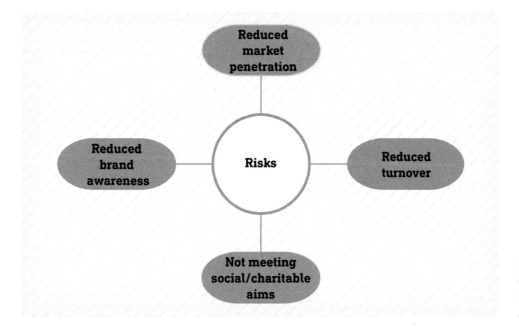

Figure 2.3: Businesses can face a range of problems if their ideas are not enterprising enough

Reduced turnover

Turnover is the revenue generated from selling products. It is calculated using the following formula:

Turnover = Number of sales × price of the product or service

A lack of enterprise could mean that the business's products or services will not remain as popular as they once were. If other competitors start to operate in the market, sales figures may fall, reducing turnover further. This will ultimately mean that the business will make less profit and may even struggle to meet its costs.

Reduced market penetration

MARKET PENETRATION involves either increasing market share in the original market or entering new markets. For example, a business could increase its share of a market from 10 per cent to 15 per cent, or it could enter a new market by starting to sell in another country. A lack of enterprise, such as failing to develop new products or redevelop products that are declining in popularity, could mean that the business loses some of its share in the market or struggles to expand into new markets.

Reduced brand awareness

Brand awareness is the process of creating a strong brand image. A lack of enterprise may mean that the product or service becomes outdated or people are less aware of it. This will reduce brand awareness, and the enterprise idea may become less successful.

Not meeting social or charitable aims

Today, it is important that businesses set themselves social aims. These are aims focused on the interests of the public and other people, to ensure that others are not negatively affected by the actions of the business. These can include environmental aims, and aims to ethically source products or raw materials and treat their workers fairly.

Many firms also set themselves charitable aims, identifying charities to associate themselves with and raise money for. A lack of enterprise may mean that the business becomes short of money and so may focus on making as much as possible, without considering its social/charitable aims. This could negatively affect the business's image and reputation.

Weighing the risks and benefits

All these risks could result in the business losing market share and profit. You need to carefully weigh the benefits of enterprise against the risks of lack of enterprise.

How could a supermarket increase its market share?

Ready for assessment

For your assignment, you will need to explain and evaluate the features of successful enterprise ideas.

1 Select two products or services that have been successful and explain which of the successful features they have (see Figure 2.2), and how they have generated them.

2 Evaluate these features. This involves explaining which features have been most important and how much they have contributed to the overall success of the enterprise idea.

3 Analyse how the entrepreneurs behind these products and services have developed and implemented their enterprise ideas.

4 Identify the benefits and risks of enterprise. List these under each of the headings of 'Benefits of enterprise' and 'Risks of enterprise'. You can then use your list in your assignment work for this learning aim.

5 Now create your own idea for a product or service for a new business start-up. Explain the features that make it successful and their contribution to the start-up's success.

Benefits of enterprise	Risks of enterprise

Skills and knowledge check

- [ ] What is the difference between an entrepreneur and an intrapreneur?
- [ ] At which point of the product life cycle would you be likely to withdraw a product or service?
- [ ] Name three features of a successful enterprise idea.
- [ ] What risks are associated with a lack of enterprise?

- ◯ I can explain each stage of the product life cycle.
- ◯ I understand what features make an enterprise successful.
- ◯ I can identify the different enterprise skills needed to make an enterprise idea successful.

B Generate enterprise ideas using creativity techniques

When generating enterprise ideas, creativity is important for spotting opportunities.

B1 Creativity techniques

You can use several techniques to stimulate your creativity.

TGROW (topic, goal, reality, options, will)

TGROW involves the following stages to generate and develop an enterprise idea.

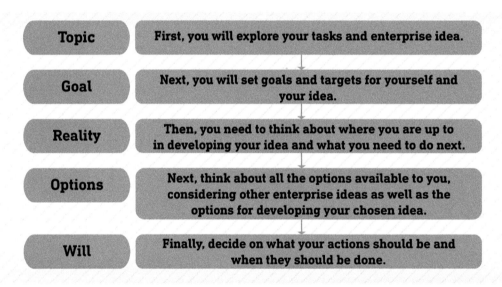

Topic	First, you will explore your tasks and enterprise idea.
Goal	Next, you will set goals and targets for yourself and your idea.
Reality	Then, you need to think about where you are up to in developing your idea and what you need to do next.
Options	Next, think about all the options available to you, considering other enterprise ideas as well as the options for developing your chosen idea.
Will	Finally, decide on what your actions should be and when they should be done.

Figure 2.4: Using TGROW to progress your enterprise idea

STEP BY STEP TGROW

Checklist: Use this checklist to complete TGROW about your enterprise idea

Topic	Goal	Reality	Options	Will
☐ What is the task? ☐ What do I have to produce? ☐ What are my ideas?	☐ What is the goal of the activity? ☐ What are the aims of the idea?	☐ What have I done so far? ☐ What is still left to be done? ☐ What do I need to do next?	☐ What other ideas do I have? ☐ What can I do to change the idea? ☐ What changes should I make?	☐ What needs to be done now? ☐ What actions should I take? ☐ What order should I do them in?
STEP 1 Explore the tasks and the enterprise idea	**STEP 2** Set goals and targets for myself and the idea	**STEP 3** Think about where I am with the idea and what else I need to do	**STEP 4** Think about the options I have to change my idea	**STEP 5** Make a list of what I need to do now

Imagine and visualise success

This is a technique used to make ideas successful. It is commonly used in sport. It involves creating and rehearsing a positive mental experience to enhance the ability to achieve a successful outcome in real life. This is also important when you prepare for and carry out a pitch of your enterprise idea. Imagining success may make you feel more confident, so you can express your ideas in a more convincing and persuasive way.

The journalistic six

You can use the 'JOURNALISTIC SIX' to crystallise your vision of your idea. It involves asking six questions – who, what, where, when, why and how – about the enterprise idea. The objective here is to think through every aspect of the idea, to identify all potential problems and refine your idea to avoid them.

For example, think about the following questions when using the journalistic six.

1 *Who* will be responsible for each task that needs to be carried out? Will you need more employees to make the idea successful?
2 *What* exactly is the idea? What will it do? What will it include?
3 *Where* will the idea be based? Where will you sell it? Where will you buy it from? Where will you make it?
4 *When*: how long will it take to create? In what order will you do the tasks you need to do? When will you launch the idea? When will it start to make a profit? When will you sell it?
5 *Why*: for every decision made and action taken, think about why you are doing it. Does it have to be done that way? Is it vital to the enterprise idea? Also, what are your aims and objectives?
6 *How* will you achieve each of the tasks that need doing? How will you let people know about your idea? How will you make it successful? How will you know it is successful?

SWOT analysis

Businesses regularly use a SWOT analysis to help them think about all the variables involved and to weigh up the positive and negative aspects. They will list current strengths and weaknesses alongside future opportunities and threats. They then use this list to make decisions.

Mind mapping

You may have used MIND MAPPING before. This is where ideas are organised into a diagram where they are placed in order or grouped under common headings.

Figure 2.5: Noting down risks, strengths, options and the people involved in a mind map will help you organise your thoughts

Visualisation

VISUALISATION is a technique you can use to create an image of your final enterprise idea. It involves visualising the idea from all angles, allowing you to consider all aspects relating to it. You can also identify potential problems and create solutions to them.

Storytelling

STORYTELLING involves verbalising your ideas, explaining to others exactly what you plan to do, how you are going to do it and what the outcome will be. This can then be extended to encourage others to offer their suggestions and ideas for improvement.

Lateral thinking

LATERAL THINKING involves the ability to think creatively, or 'outside the box'. You need to use your inspiration and imagination to solve problems by looking at each problem from different angles. For example, when creating a new enterprise idea, such as a new dog grooming business, it would be useful to think about all the products and services that could possibly be sold. Also, consider the idea from the point of view of different people such as different dog owners, local residents and suppliers.

Link it up

In Unit 4 you will plan and pitch your idea. So, before you do this, it would be useful to encourage others to offer their suggestions and ideas, so that you can gather feedback and advice before you complete your pitch.

Encouraging others to offer suggestions and ideas

It is useful to get feedback and advice on your enterprise idea. So explain your idea to others, and encourage them to offer their suggestions and ideas. It is also useful to get advice from other mentors and business forums about your idea, and reflect on the feedback given to you. You could present your idea and pitch to local entrepreneurs or business people to gather their feedback. Businesses also constantly ask for feedback from the public. Walkers has run a number of high-profile campaigns asking customers to vote on which flavours of crisps they want to see on the market. Most recently, it has created flavour A and flavour B of its Doritos brand; flavour A, Sizzling Salsa, was the winner and joined the Doritos range.

Practise

Try one of the following suggestions:

- produce a mind map for your enterprise idea, developing your ideas
- use the storytelling technique, by explaining your ideas to a partner (you could also encourage them to offer suggestions and ideas)
- practise the journalistic six technique for your enterprise idea
- imagine and visualise success by writing down your ambitions for your enterprise idea and where it will be in 10 years.

Link it up

To remind yourself about the needs of the business environment, look back at A3 earlier in this unit.

In Unit 1, learning aim B, you will have already examined the external environment and its impact on the development and implementation of enterprise ideas.

Later in this unit (C2) you will examine appropriate market research techniques to help you gather the information you need.

B2 Refining enterprise ideas

When you have generated your enterprise idea, you will need to assess whether it will contribute to the success of the business. Consider each of the following contributions.

Meeting market needs

Does your idea meet the needs of its **TARGET MARKET** (the type of customer you hope to attract)? It is important to carry out market research to find out what people want, and then refine your enterprise idea to reflect this.

Practise

Think about and research the business environment, and identify gaps in the market. You will have to look again at your idea and adapt it so that it meets the needs of the business environment.

Increasing turnover

Think about how much turnover your enterprise idea will generate, and how you could increase the amount.

Increasing brand awareness

Examine whether your enterprise idea will create a strong brand, and think about how you will ensure that customers are aware of it.

What if...?

Andy has just left college after studying for a Level 2 qualification in business. He has recently been given £7,000 by his grandparents to help him to start his own business. He has always wanted to set up his own business based on his interest in animals and has decide to open a dog grooming salon.

1 Why is it important that Andy generates a number of enterprise ideas to consider before launching his dog grooming salon?

2 What techniques would be useful for him to use to generate and refine his enterprise ideas?

Link it up

In Unit 3 (A2), you will learn more about turnover and branding. You can use that information to help you here.

Increasing social capital

SOCIAL CAPITAL means the connections between people and organisations, and the creation of mutually advantageous projects and outcomes. It is important to assess the impact of your enterprise idea on other people and other businesses, and how it could benefit both you and them. An important aspect of creating social capital is using professional networking. It is increasingly done online through social media sites like LinkedIn.

Practise

In learning aim A in this unit, you created a list of new products or services for a market or industry of your choice. Choose three of the enterprise ideas. For each idea, assess how it will contribute to the factors listed on this page and page 63. Remember: 'assessing' involves thinking about how the idea contributes, and how significant the contribution is, to the business.

When you have assessed how enterprise ideas contribute to the success of the business, you will need to be able to select a good, credible enterprise idea. Also ensure that you are able to give reasons explaining why you have rejected the other ideas.

Ready for assessment

To help prepare for your assignment, write notes under each of the headings below.

'The techniques I have used to develop my enterprise ideas'

'An assessment of how three enterprise ideas could contribute to the success of the business'

'Reasons for selecting this enterprise idea and how I know it is credible'

'Reasons for discounting the other two enterprise ideas'.

To achieve the higher marks for this assessment, you will also need to use the market research you are about to gather in the next learning aim of this unit to refine and assess your enterprise idea further to meet the needs of its target market. To do this, you will need to use the skills and knowledge you have gained both from this learning aim and the next learning aim of this unit.

Skills and knowledge check

- [ ] What are the different stages of the TGROW technique?
- [ ] What does visualisation involve?
- [ ] How can refining an enterprise idea help it meet the needs of the business environment?

- ( ) I can explain all the different techniques that can be used to stimulate creativity.
- ( ) I understand how refining an enterprise idea can contribute to increased turnover.

C Investigate market research for a selected enterprise idea

To make sure an enterprise idea is successful, it is important to carry out high-quality research into the market.

C1 Develop research based on the needs of the four Ps

Before you carry out any research, you need to be aware of the needs of the **FOUR PS**.

The marketing mix and the four Ps

The four Ps are the main components of the marketing mix for a product or service. The marketing mix is designed to let potential customers know about the enterprise idea, provide information and persuade them to buy the product or service. It consists of:

1 *price* – the price that will be charged to customers
2 *promotion* – all the methods used to attract potential customers or ensure that customers return to buy the product or service
3 *place* – how and where the product or service is sold or provided
4 *product* – the design, functionality and construction of the product or service.

Seven Ps

You may also find the **SEVEN PS** mentioned in some textbooks. This adds the following to the four Ps:

5 *physical evidence* – how a business and its products are perceived by its customers and the general public
6 *people* – staff working for the organisation, their customer service skills and the positive image they portray of the business
7 *process* – the processes and systems used to provide or deliver the good or service to the customer.

Some other marketers even talk about the 10 Ps. However, within your assignment work, it is sufficient to focus on the four Ps.

Utilising the four Ps

In your assignment, you will need to research the four Ps in connection with successful enterprise ideas, and suggest ways that you will use the four Ps in your enterprise idea. You will need to make sure that you think about price, product, promotion and place together to ensure that your enterprise idea can be successful. For example, you may have the perfect product or service in the right place at the right price, but promote it in the entirely wrong way. Or you may have an excellent promotional campaign, but the price you are charging is not enough to cover the costs.

Price and pricing strategies

When introducing a new enterprise idea, it is vital that the product or service has the correct price. Charging a price that is too high will result in a lack of demand for the product or service. On the other hand, charging a price that is too low will mean that profit is lost, resulting in the enterprise idea not being successful.

There are several ways to decide the correct price to charge for a product or service.

- **PENETRATION** – charging a low price initially, to encourage people to try the product and to establish brand loyalty. Over time, the price is increased to make more profit.
- **SKIMMING** – charging a high price initially, to skim off as much profit as possible. Over time, the price is reduced.
- **COMPETITOR-BASED** – before the price is set, the price of competitors' products or services is considered. This usually results in charging the same price as competitors.
- **COST PLUS** – calculating the break-even price for the product by adding material costs, direct labour costs and other expenses. Then, based on the profit the business needs to make, a percentage is added to the final price charged to customers.
- **MARK UP** – the percentage that you are adding to the break-even cost of the product or service in cost-plus pricing. It ensures that a consistent level of profit is made.

Table 2.1: Comparing different types of pricing

Cost-plus pricing	Mark-up pricing
Material costs = £20	Variable costs = £20
Direct labour costs = £16	Fixed cost per unit = £40
Other expenses = £14	Total cost per unit = £60
Direct costs = £50	Mark up % = 30%
Profit % = 25%	Mark up = £18
Profit required = £12.50	Price charged = £78
Price charged = £62.50	

Link it up

In Unit 3, learning aim C, you will learn more about financing an enterprise idea.

Promotion

Promotion is used to make customers aware of a product or service that has been produced from the initial enterprise idea. If people are not aware of the product or service and its USPs, they will not be willing to buy it, and so the enterprise idea will not be successful. Creating brand awareness is important for generating sales. For example, the Emirates Group sponsors Arsenal Football Club to ensure that its company name is seen by millions of people every time the team plays. Alternatively, many companies, such as Tesco, are now using a combination of '**BRICKS AND CLICKS**', which involves using both the internet and physical stores to sell their products.

Practise

Write a list of all the methods you could use to promote your enterprise idea. What types of media could you use?

Figure 2.6: Using the promotional mix will maximise exposure for your product or service

- *Advertising* – adverts can be placed in newspapers, magazines, at bus stops, and so on, to promote the product or service.
- *Public relations (PR)* – spreading awareness of the product or service to the public through different forms of media.
- *Sponsorship* – a business pays to have its product or service linked to a specific event or person.
- *Social media* – social media is the name for a range of online platforms, including Facebook and Twitter. These and other media can also be used for advertising and promotion.
- *Personal selling* – face-to-face selling to persuade a customer to buy the product or service.

Personal selling is still a very effective promotional tool, even in the face of the many new technologies used for promotion

Link it up

In Unit 3, you will analyse the strengths and weaknesses of promotional methods for an enterprise idea and produce a promotional plan for your idea. You can use the knowledge and skills developed here in Unit 2 to help you complete your evidence for Unit 3.

- *Digital marketing* – marketing a product or service by using digital technologies including the internet, mobile phones, digital display advertising, and any other digital medium.
- *Bricks and clicks* – using both physical shops and the internet to sell the product or service.

Place

Deciding how and where to sell the product or service is important when creating an enterprise idea. Many **DISTRIBUTION CHANNELS** (the places, and methods, through which customers can buy from you) can be used:

- **RETAIL** – selling small quantities to a customer who will use the product or service themselves. Examples include shops and market stalls.
- **WHOLESALE** – selling large quantities to retailers which then sell the product or service on to customers.
- **WEBSITE** – selling products to the customer via the company's own website.
- **THIRD-PARTY WEBSITES** – selling products to the customer via other business's websites, such as Amazon and eBay.

Practise

Choose a well-known product or service. Research where and how the product or service is sold. Put the different methods and places under the four headings above.

B2B and B2C businesses

- Businesses also need to consider whether their customers are consumers or other businesses, or both.
- **BUSINESS TO BUSINESS (B2B)** – a business that sells its product or service to other businesses.
- **BUSINESS TO CONSUMER (B2C)** – a business that sells its product or service to consumers.

A different type of approach may be needed depending on whether you are selling to consumers or other businesses. Businesses may place much bigger orders, for example, but will often take a lot longer to make a decision about whether to buy at all.

Product (or service)

Ensuring that you have created a product or service that meets the needs of your customers is important in creating an enterprise idea. You have already considered this earlier in this unit when you refined your enterprise idea. When creating your product, think about what it does, what it feels like, how it works and what it looks like. For example, when creating the iPhone 7, Apple considered, among other factors: the size of the product; the colour; the way it functions; the tasks it performs; and how the logo could be used to promote the brand.

Practise

What did you consider to ensure that your product or service would meet the needs of your customers?

In creating a product or service for your enterprise idea, you need to consider:

USP (UNIQUE SELLING POINT) – the factor or factors that make a product or service different to all the others on the market. For example, the way the product looks or the way it works.

Packaging – the box or packet your product is sold in must attract the attention of the customer. Important factors to consider are colour, essential information and the product logo. It is also useful to think about other types of packaging such as the shopping bags customers will use to take their purchased products from the store.

Brand image – creating a brand image is important. A brand is a product or service that is distinctive and easily recognisable from others on the market. Examples of strong brands include Dyson, Heinz and Adidas.

Can you think of any products, other than children's toys, that have obvious 'personalities'?

Personality – when creating a product, it is vital to try to give it its own 'personality'. This includes thinking about the target customers and trying to make the product match their personality. For example, an Apple iPhone can be adapted with different covers and screen settings according to each customer's preferences.

Ready for assessment

For your assignment, you will need to look at how products or services similar to your own enterprise idea use the four Ps. You then need to think about how you would use the four Ps in creating your enterprise idea.

Research similar businesses. Write down the things you like and dislike about their products or services, and make a note of the aspects of the products or services you might like to use in your enterprise idea.

Choose three of the businesses and write down how they use the four Ps to market their product or service. You could use the internet to do your research, but make sure that you keep a record of the websites you have used. Be specific about what you are looking for when searching, and try to use a company's own website because it will contain accurate information.

You could also visit the three businesses and make notes on how they use the four Ps. You could talk to people who work there or the owners of the business. You could also collect photos and examples of promotional materials to provide more evidence.

Think about how their use of the four Ps will influence your use of the four Ps for your enterprise idea.

Under a heading for each of the four Ps, make some notes about your ideas. Below are some short examples to help you.

You can use your notes when preparing to complete your assignment.

Product

The product comes in a range of colours and sizes and has the company logo on it. The shop has plastic bags that are reusable and have the company name and logo on them.

Promotion

The shop has a buy-one-get-one-free offer on for the product and has this promoted on signs around the shop. It also has colourful displays outside the shop to attract customers to come in. It advertises in the local paper and I have collected an example of a leaflet that has come through my front door promoting the product.

Price

The price of the product is £19.99, which is similar to the price charged by a number of other shops in the area. Therefore, I know they are using competition pricing.

Place

You can buy the product in the store and online. The store is on the high street which is really easy to get to and a lot of people walk past every day. The business focuses on business-to-customer sales and does this through its own retailers. It pays a supplier to make the products for it.

Figure 2.7: Example of how the four Ps can be used

Link it up

In Unit 4 (A2), you will need to consider the four Ps for your enterprise idea. When planning your pitch in Unit 4, learning aim B, use the knowledge and skills you have developed in this section.

Link it up

In Unit 1 (B1), you will have examined the external operational environment and its impact on enterprise ideas. You will also have analysed the role of stakeholders, in preparing for your external assessment. Use your knowledge and experience from Unit 1 to help you in completing your market research for Unit 2.

C2 Market research methods

To make sure that there is a market for an enterprise idea before you launch the product or service, it is vital to do some market research. There is no point going to the effort of implementing your chosen marketing mix if no one will buy the product. You will need to gather information on potential customers and their ability to pay for the product or service, alongside the views and influence of other key **STAKEHOLDERS**. Stakeholders are individuals or groups who have an interest in the success of the business. Before getting started on your enterprise idea, you will also need to research your competitors and potential gaps in the market, and of course, changes to the external environment.

To gather information to support your enterprise idea, use a range of both primary and secondary research methods:

- **PRIMARY RESEARCH** – gathering new and unique research data yourself to answer a specific question.
- **SECONDARY RESEARCH** – using information previously researched by other people.

The relationship between primary and secondary research

It is important for businesses to make sure that they use a combination of primary and secondary research together. Both forms of research should support each other. However, sometimes they may also contradict each other, for example when primary research from a small sample is compared to secondary research from a much larger sample. It is therefore vital that you use both and consider what they tell you together. For example, questionnaires completed by your target market might tell you that people would only be willing to pay a maximum of £5 for your product but your secondary research into costs of raw materials could tell you that this price would not be enough to cover the cost of production.

Practise

Before you read the next section, think about what you already know about the following research methods. Consider which of the following are primary research methods and which are secondary research methods:

- online research
- visits
- market reports
- questionnaires
- government reports
- observation
- websites
- interviews
- focus groups
- surveys
- company materials.

Primary research methods

Primary research methods you could use to research your enterprise idea include the following.

Visits

To gather research you could visit a local business. You could visit local shops to review the range of products on offer or you could visit your local town centre to make a list of your competitors. Remember to write down what you have found out while you are there, so you can use it later.

Questionnaires

You could produce a **QUESTIONNAIRE**. This is a list of questions to find out people's opinions, and their likes and dislikes, relating to the product or service. You need to think carefully about what you want to find out, and write questions that will best gather this information. There is further information later in this unit to help you think about the type of questions to ask and the types of people you should question.

Observation

You could observe a local business owner or visit a local business to see how the business works, to help you think about your business idea.

Interviews

You could interview local entrepreneurs about how they created and introduced their enterprise ideas, using pre-written questions to help you. You could also interview potential customers to find out about their preferences and opinions. Remember, though, each interview provides only one person's point of view.

Focus groups

To gather more than one person's opinions, you could hold a **FOCUS GROUP**. This is where you gather a number of people and ask them specific questions about a product or a service. Remember to think about your target market, and include a range of different types of people.

Surveys

You could undertake a survey, asking people for their opinions on a number of issues. You could do this in school or college, at work or around the town you live in.

Have you ever taken a survey? How did you find the experience?

Practise

Write a list of questions you can use when you interview a local entrepreneur or business owner.

Think about what you want to know. What could the person tell you that could help to make your enterprise idea successful?

Secondary research methods

Secondary research methods that you can use to research your enterprise idea include the following.

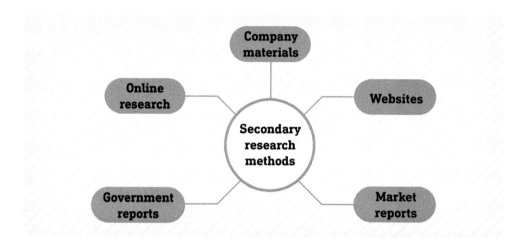

Figure 2.8: Secondary research will allow you to build on any primary research you have carried out

Online research

You can do online research to help you find out about the market, industry, customers and other competitors. Be careful when choosing where you look online. Make sure you know that the source you are using is reliable and accurate. It is always useful to double-check information with another source or website to make sure it is correct.

Websites

To gather information on companies and products or services similar to your enterprise idea, you can use their websites. But be careful. Is the website telling you about the company and product? Or is it trying to persuade you to buy the product?

Company materials

You could use a range of company materials in your research. These include financial reports, presentations to the company's SHAREHOLDERS (investors) on its website, reports and promotional material. All of this will provide you with some examples of what similar businesses to yours are doing.

Market reports

Many companies produce reports on individual markets looking at market share, turnover, product ranges, and so on. This might be useful to you in providing an overview of the market as a whole.

Government reports

The government also produces reports that you might find useful. These might look at national TRENDS (patterns that can be mapped over time), including data on population changes, unemployment rates and the growth of certain industries. This will help you to think about your external OPERATIONAL ENVIRONMENT and how this will affect your enterprise idea.

Types of question

When preparing to gather primary research such as questionnaires, focus groups or surveys, think about the types of questions that you can ask. You should use a combination of **OPEN QUESTIONS**, **CLOSED QUESTIONS** and **LIKERT SCALE QUESTIONS**.

Open questions

The response to open questions can be long and detailed, and lets the respondents say whatever they like. Examples of this type of question are 'What do you like about this pair of trainers?' and 'What do you look for when buying a new pair of trainers?'

Closed questions

The response to closed questions will be more specific, such as 'yes', 'no' or a specific number. This type of question is useful when you want to gather more precise data.

Open questions	Closed questions
Can you describe what it was about the product/service that you liked?	Did you like the product/service?
How did you find using the product/service?	Was it easy to use the product/service?
What would you change about the product/service?	Would you recommend the product/service to your friends and family?

Table 2.2: Examples of different types of questions

Likert scale questions

The response to Likert scale questions will be on a scale from one to five. The respondents are asked to think about key factors of a product or service and rate them by order of preference. For example, you might ask your sample of people to think about different types of shoe styles and rate them with either 'dislike a lot', 'dislike', 'no preference', 'like' or 'like a lot'.

	Dislike a lot	Dislike	No preference	Like	Like a lot
How do you feel about the new chocolate flavour?	O	O	O	O	O

Figure 2.9: Likert scale questions ask respondents to consider key factors and rate them either by number or the extent to which they like a product or agree with a statement

Using a range of different types of questions can help you to carry out both **QUALITATIVE RESEARCH** and **QUANTITATIVE RESEARCH**.

Qualitative research

Qualitative research methods measure how people feel, what they think and why they make certain choices. This would involve asking open questions through questionnaires, surveys or focus groups. You will want to gather some quite detailed information, so you will need to give people plenty of time to think about their answers and explain them to you.

Quantitative research

Quantitative methods measure what people think from a statistical and numerical point of view. For example, you could ask people how many products they buy and how often. Or you could research how sales have changed in a particular market.

The relationship between qualitative and quantitative research

You might use qualitative research to support the quantitative research you have done. For example, you might have gathered information on how many people would be willing to buy your product or service at certain prices in your quantitative research, but then you want to find out why and what would encourage them to buy more. It is important to gather both facts and figures, and people's feelings and opinions to help you understand their responses and to find out more. You might also find that your research leads to further questions. If it does, you might need to follow it up with more research, such as an interview or a focus group.

Practise

Write a questionnaire to use in either a survey or a focus group to gather potential customers' views on your enterprise idea. Use a range of different types of questions to help you gather both qualitative and quantitative data.

Link it up 🔗

In the final section of this unit (C4), you will find information on how to present and interpret qualitative and quantitative data.

Sample size and reliability

You need to think about the type of people you choose for your research, based on the target market of your enterprise idea. The people you ask to participate in your research are called the **SAMPLE**. You need to think about how many people you need to ask. You do not want too many people, because you might get too much information to cope with. However, you also need enough people to ensure that your research is not dominated by the views of a few of the people.

You need your research to be reliable. If you focus on groups of people who are too similar, or who are not in your target market, this will provide you with unreliable research.

Practise

Select a sample for your survey or focus group. When considering your sample, think about who your target market is. What ages are they? Do they include men and women? Are you targeting your product to a certain level of income?

Identifying and reducing bias

Make sure that you use a range of different types of customer, to help you ensure that your research is reliable and that it is not **BIASED**. Bias is a tendency to favour one particular group or opinion.

It is important to choose reliable sources of secondary research. Avoid using sources that may be biased or that provide unreliable evidence. You need to think about who has published the research. Are they an official, reliable source of information?

Practise

Write a list of all the sources you could use to undertake secondary research for your enterprise idea. What will they tell you? How reliable and valid are they? What is the risk of bias?

Ready for assessment

For your assignment, you will need to use a range of market research methods relevant to your target market to research your enterprise idea. You will need to gather information on customers' views and demands, competitors' products and the external operational environment.

List at least three primary research methods and three secondary research methods that you could use.

Remember, you can choose from the following lists:

Table 2.3: Primary and secondary research methods

Primary research	Secondary research
Visits	Online research
Questionnaires	Websites
Observation	Company materials
Interviews	Market reports
Focus groups	Government reports
Surveys	

Carry out the research, gathering together all the information and data that you will use in your assignment work.

Organise your research under the headings of 'customer views and demands', 'competitor products' and 'external environment'. Make sure you include what the research has told you and where it was from.

C3 Data presentation and interpretation

When you have gathered your research, you will need to present the data in an appropriate format and interpret what it means. It is important, when presenting an enterprise idea, that you present the information in a professional and interesting way. It is also vital that you interpret the data you have gathered, to help you make decisions about how to refine your enterprise idea.

Using appropriate methods to present your findings

You will need to use all the information you have gathered to present your findings. Remember that the purpose of your market research is to develop and refine your enterprise idea for your target market. You could use the following headings to organise your findings and present them in a professional and business-like manner.

Using headings

Introduction

Explain what your enterprise idea is and who your target market is going to be. This will set the scene for your findings.

Methods used

Explain the methods you have used, providing references for any sources you used.

Link it up

In Unit 4 (B1), you will present your enterprise idea, so you might want to use some of the techniques described in this section to help you there.

Findings

Explain what you found and what this tells you about your enterprise idea. Your findings can be presented in several different ways – some suggestions have been provided later in this section of the unit.

Conclusions

Summarise and come up with conclusions based on what you have found. Write about how your findings will affect your enterprise idea. At this point you may need to refine your enterprise idea further. Remember to match this again to your target market.

There is an example of a report layout below to help you.

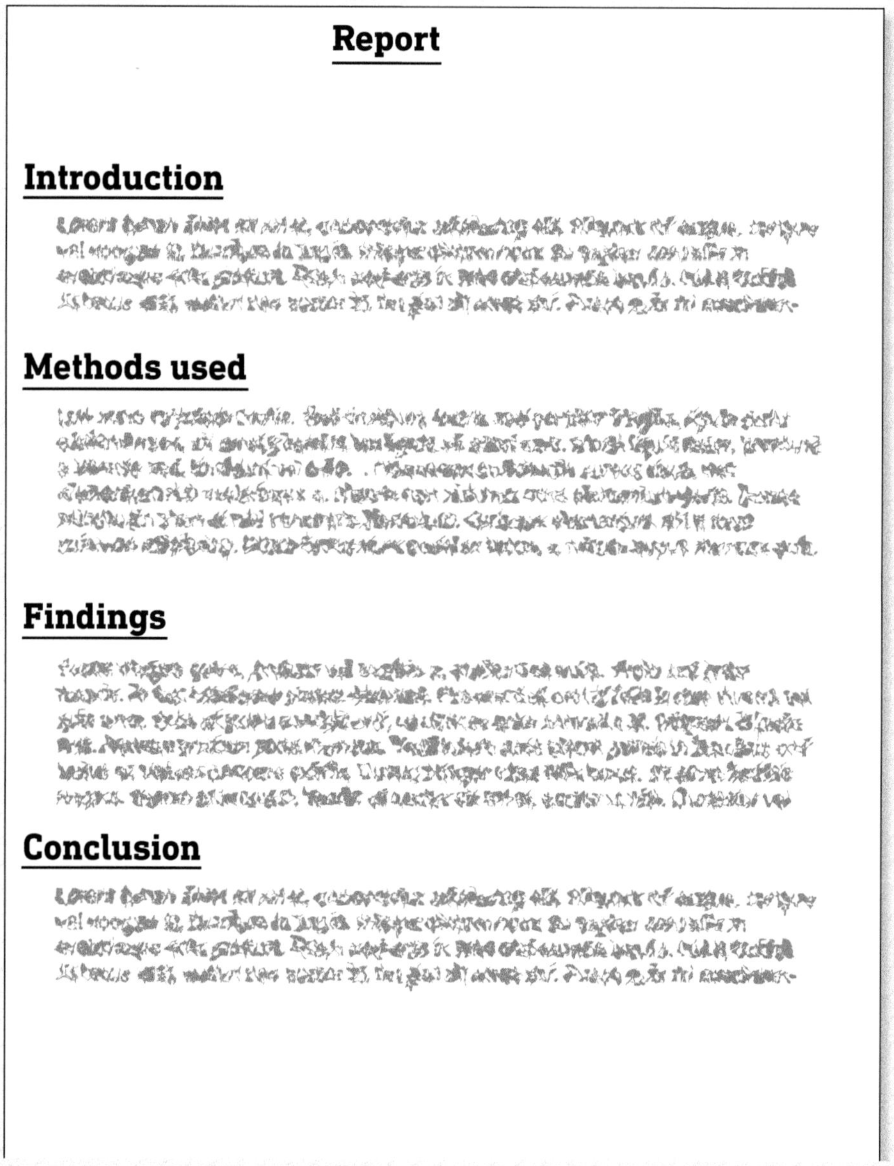

Figure 2.10: Laying out a report in a professional-looking way

Link it up

Look back to the section on 'Refining enterprise ideas' (B2) to help you refine your idea further.

Using presentation methods

You will need to use a range of different presentation methods to present your findings, depending on the type of research. Here are some suggestions of methods you could use.

Charts

Charts and tables are good ways of summarising a lot of quantitative data. You could use these to summarise the outcomes of primary research such as questionnaires, surveys and focus groups, but also data from secondary research, such as government reports.

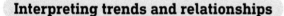

Bar chart   **Pie chart**   **Scatter graph**

Figure 2.11: Charts and graphs can make your data look more visual

Graphs

Graphs are a good way of presenting a lot of data in one place. They can help you to identify trends and relationships between different variables.

Calculations

You will find it useful to calculate percentages when you are analysing quantitative data generated from primary research such as questionnaires, surveys and focus groups.

Practise

Use your secondary research to produce a SWOT analysis and a PESTEL analysis, based on the external environment related to your enterprise idea. Think about the market, any potential gaps in the market and the competition.

What do your analyses tell you about the likelihood of your enterprise idea being successful?

Link it up

In Unit 1 (B1), you examined the external environment and you used both PESTEL and SWOT analyses to explain the impact of the external environment on the success of enterprise. Use this work from Unit 1 to help you here.

Interpreting trends and relationships

When you have presented your data in a suitable format, you will need to interpret the trends in the data and the relationships between different variables in the sets of data. You need to look at your charts or graphs and identify any trends in the data. For example: Has the data increased or decreased over time? Has the data changed a lot across the data set? Are there any major similarities or differences between different types of customers?

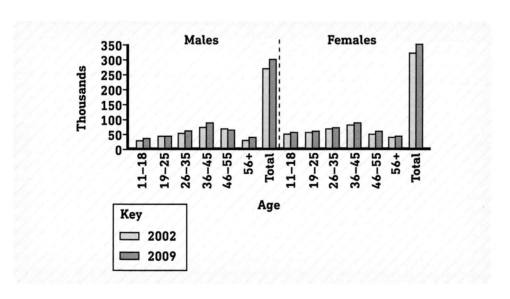

Figure 2.12: Breaking down data by gender and age range

Here is an example of how you might interpret the data in the bar chart in Figure 2.12.

- Have the numbers sold increased or decreased between 2002 and 2009? For both men and women, the numbers sold have increased from 2002 and 2009. The number bought by men has increased from 260,000 to 290,000 and for women it has increased from 315,000 to 334,000. This tells us there is more demand for the product.
- Which age range buys most of the products? For both men and women the groups that buy most of the product are 36–45-year-olds, followed by 46–55-year-old men and 26–35-year-old women. This means that this is the target market for the product.
- Who buys more of the products? Women buy more of the product than men do over all age groups, and women bought 44,000 more of the product than men in 2009. This means that women and men should be targeted, but women should be targeted more than men.

When you have interpreted the trends and relationships in your data set, you will need to think about what the data is telling you about your enterprise idea.

What if...?

Look at the graph below.

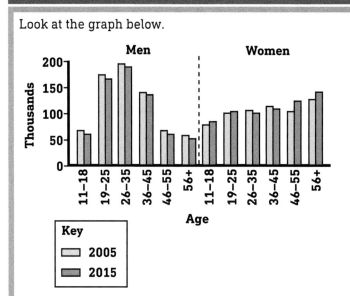

Figure 2.13: Number of items bought broken down by age and gender

Identify where there are trends and relationships between the different variables in the data set.

1 Are there any differences between men and women?

2 Where are the similarities and differences in the data set across different ages?

3 What has happened over the period 2005–15?

Now imagine this is based on your product or service a year after it was launched.

1 What do the trends in the data set tell you about your enterprise idea?

2 Does the data tell you that people would like to buy your product or service?

3 Will you now need to refine your enterprise idea based on the data?

4 Does the data indicate that your enterprise idea has been successful?

Ready for assessment

Look at all the market research you have gathered during the practice activities throughout this unit.

1 Present each piece of research in an appropriate format. Use the information provided earlier in this unit to help you decide what format to use.

2 Write a short statement to justify why you have presented the research in your chosen format.

3 Interpret each piece of research. Include the following aspects to help you to do this effectively.

- What does the research tell you?

- What does that mean for your enterprise idea?

- Does the research support your enterprise idea?

- Do you need to refine your enterprise idea in light of the research?

4 Overall, explain what all the research tells you and how this affects your enterprise idea. Have you changed your enterprise idea? How will you refine it?

Skills and knowledge check

☐ What is the marketing mix?

☐ Can you list five different forms of promotion?

☐ What is a USP?

☐ What pricing strategies can you use to price a product or service?

◯ I have researched how a successful business uses place in the four Ps.

◯ I know why the four Ps are important to research when generating an enterprise idea.

◯ I can use computer software to draw a range of graphs.

◯ I can organise my market research into a professional and business-like format.

◯ I can interpret data sets, identifying trends and relationships between variables.

◯ I can make decisions about my enterprise idea based on data sets.

WORK FOCUS

HANDS ON

There are some important skills and techniques that you will need to practise that relate to this unit. Developing these and practising them could help you in preparing to work as an entrepreneur.

Create successful enterprise ideas

- Look for successful enterprise ideas in your workplace, and note down their features.

- Look at ideas that might not be working well in your workplace, and consider the reasons why.

Demonstrate enterprise skills

- Look for problems in your workplace.

- Practise looking for solutions to the problems.

- Examine the products you make or sell in your workplace, and look for gaps in the market.

Generate and refine enterprise ideas

- Practise using the different techniques that can be used to generate ideas based on any

decisions you have to make at work, in your personal life or in college.

- When you have used these techniques, discuss how successfully they worked for you with a friend, colleague or supervisor.

Use the four Ps to market an enterprise idea

- Look for the four Ps in your workplace, and consider how they can be improved.

Gather and use market research

- Practise writing questions and asking people their opinions in your workplace.

- Use websites to find out information you need, such as routes to work or information on potential employers.

Interpret data

- Look into research that has already been produced and practise interpreting what it means.

- Write reports based on your day at work.

Ready for work?

Do this short quiz to find out whether you would make a successful entrepreneur.

1 On deciding what enterprise idea to choose, you should:

- [ ] A Develop all the options and then decide.
- [ ] B Focus on one idea and develop it.
- [ ] C Ask other people's opinions on each idea before deciding.
- [ ] D Pick the first idea you come up with.

2 When refining an enterprise idea, you should:

- [ ] A Consider the strengths and weaknesses of the idea.
- [ ] B Look at what was good and ignore the rest.
- [ ] C Use creativity techniques to reassess and refine the idea.
- [ ] D Go with the idea anyway because you think it is a good idea.

3 When undertaking secondary research:

- [ ] A Use a range of websites checking they are correct.
- [ ] B Use the websites of businesses you know a lot about.
- [ ] C Use a number of sources to double-check the information is correct.
- [ ] D Use the first website you come across.

4 When using primary research, it is important to:

- [ ] A Use a range of techniques to make sure the information is accurate.
- [ ] B Ask your friends and family for their opinions.
- [ ] C Think carefully about selecting the right people to match the target market.
- [ ] D Write down your own opinions, because you know what people think.

5 When presenting your ideas and research:

- [ ] A Make notes under key headings with your reasons for the decisions you made.
- [ ] B Outline the enterprise idea and explain why you think it will work.
- [ ] C Produce a detailed, professionally presented report.
- [ ] D Write down the decision made and your reasons for it.

Your score:

A = 2; B = 3; C = 4; D = 1

If you scored mostly As, you may need to brush up on your enterprise skills. Mostly Bs, go back and read the relevant learning aim of the unit. Mostly Cs, you have a good understanding of the skills involved. Mostly Ds, you need to revisit the content in this unit.

3 Promoting and Financing an Enterprise Idea

When working on an enterprise idea, you need to think about how you will both promote and finance your idea. In this unit, you will discover the different types of promotion you can use and which might be best for your enterprise. You will also learn about the best ways of financing your idea, and the factors you will need to consider.

What types of promotional activity do you see every day? Which types attract you more than others? Have you ever thought about how businesses fund their promotional activities? Or how they fund their entire enterprise?

How will I be assessed?

This is a practical unit. You will develop a promotional campaign for a product or service as part of your enterprise idea. After identifying the strengths and weaknesses of a variety of promotional methods, you will use a set of promotional targets to justify your choice of promotional methods. You will then demonstrate your skills and knowledge by putting together a plan for your promotional campaign.

You will also produce a financial plan, which will later form part of your business plan. In your financial plan, you will analyse the predicted impact of the costs and income on the cash flow of your enterprise idea and any profits likely to be made. You will use the knowledge you have gathered to consider how you will source the raw materials you will need for your business, the costs involved and the viability of your plans.

Assessment criteria

Pass	Merit	Distinction
Learning aim A: Investigate the appropriateness of promotional methods for an enterprise idea		
A.P1 Identify the strengths and weaknesses of different promotional methods for an enterprise idea.	**A.M1** Analyse the strengths and weaknesses of different promotional methods for an enterprise idea.	**AB.D1** Produce a detailed promotional plan for an enterprise idea that explains how promotional objectives will be achieved.
Learning aim B: Produce a promotional plan for the enterprise idea		
B.P2 Produce an outline promotional plan, selecting appropriate promotional methods for the enterprise idea.	**B.M2** Produce a promotional plan for the enterprise idea that links promotional methods to promotional objectives.	
Learning aim C: Produce a financial plan for the enterprise idea		
C.P3 Prepare an outline financial plan for the enterprise idea using estimates of costs and projected sales.	**C.M3** Analyse the impact of costs and revenue on cash flow and profit for the enterprise idea.	**C.D2** Evaluate the viability of the financial plan for the enterprise idea.
C.P4 Explain the factors included in an effective supply chain for the enterprise idea.		

A Investigate the appropriateness of promotional methods for the enterprise idea

In this section, you will investigate how appropriate different **PROMOTIONAL** methods are for your enterprise idea.

A1 Promotional methods including digital and online media resources as well as traditional methods

Businesses use a wide variety of ways to promote their products or services.

Selecting appropriate techniques

Businesses select the promotional techniques that they will use, depending on their products or services and their **TARGET MARKET**.

Advertising

Advertising is a promotional method that might include digital and online media resources, as well as more traditional methods such as radio, TV and advertising posters.

Internet/websites

These might include the following.

- *Website banners*: pictures or videos that are strategically placed on a **WEBSITE**.
- *Cookies*: files that store website users' browser history. Website banners can then be targeted at individual users based on the user's information stored in the cookies.
- *Pop-up screens on websites*: these might invite the user to take action, such as to subscribe to a business's newsletter, or gives the user a message such as 'Are you sure you want to leave this site?'. Pop-ups are not usually targeted to individual users.

Careful consideration needs to be given to which internet promotional methods will be the most effective. Website users have become used to website banners and pop-ups, and there are even applications (apps) to block them.

Practise

Make a list of five examples of where you have experienced the use of cookies, banners and pop-ups.

1 What was the website promoting?

2 How effective was its promotional message? Did it make you want to buy its products or services?

Social media

Social media, for example Facebook, Twitter and Instagram, is used daily by thousands of people around the world. Less well-known examples are Swarm and Pinterest. Each of these has its own advantages and disadvantages as a promotional technique.

Apps and links to other promoters

Many social media platforms are available as mobile apps, as well as more traditional websites. This means that social media promotions can be seen on a variety of devices such as desktop computers, smartphones and computer tablets. Within apps and websites there might be links that take the user to other promoters when they are clicked on. These links provide a source of income to the app and website providers, and take the user to new areas where other businesses are advertising.

Practise
Make a list of 10 different social media platforms.
1 Why would someone use each on your list?
2 How could a new business benefit from each on your list?

	Advantages	Disadvantages
Social media	• Used by many people of all ages • Has a global presence • A business can be specific with the promotional message • Can customise promotion to the target audience • Cost per lead is low • Success rate likely to be greater than traditional marketing methods	• Not everyone uses social media • Customers could become irritated with constant bombardment of advertising • May miss target market if promotion has not been thought through

Table 3.1: Advantages and disadvantages of social media

	Advantages	Disadvantages
Apps	• Easy for the user to download and operate from a smartphone • Often free to the user • Many potential customers own a smartphone • People use smartphones and other devices to fill in their time, for example when waiting for an appointment	• The business has to rely on the customer downloading the app • There are development costs to the business in creating the app • Apps may need to be updated regularly at a cost to the business

Table 3.2: Advantages and disadvantages of apps

Print media

Newspapers and magazines can be an expensive method of promotion. The business needs to consider the cost of the promotion against the amount of exposure and sales that may be obtained.

Newspaper and magazine advertisements can be eye catching, if used appropriately

Broadcast media

Television might include local TV or national TV, depending on whether the business wants to reach the whole country or target a local area. TV advertising is expensive, so the business must consider the value of using this type of promotion and the benefits to the business.

Radio advertising is used on commercial channels, both national and local. Local radio can be affordable to businesses for promoting their products or services in a local area. The business should consider who is likely to be listening to the station and if these people are their target audience.

Outdoor advertising

Advertising outdoors can include billboards on buildings or purpose-built hoardings, in public areas such as the Underground, or on commercial vehicles such as taxis and buses.

Outdoor advertising is an effective promotional technique

Practise

Think of at least two examples of the different promotion methods that have been mentioned in this section. Think of an example of the most appropriate use of each promotional example you have identified, and discuss with a partner or in a group:

1 Who are the customers likely to be for each promotional example?

2 Is the cost likely to be large or small to the business?

3 How would you be able to find out more about the promotional examples you have identified?

Promotional marketing

Businesses might choose to use promotions as a way of marketing their products or services. This can be face-to-face contact with their customers or remotely through the internet or telephone sales. Each type of promotional marketing technique is used with a particular aim in mind, to support a business in a number of ways in its marketing campaign. Using the right technique is important to maximise profit and minimise the cost of the promotion.

Short-term special offers

Businesses use short-term special offers to entice customers to try out their products or services. This may be an introductory special price, a free gift or free credit. Businesses might use short-term special offers during expected quiet periods for the business, or as a new opening offer if the business is new.

Point-of-sale displays

Customers might buy on impulse at the point (the location) at which they will pay for their product and/or service – this is called the **POINT OF SALE**. By carefully selecting the products and services to promote at the point of sale, a business can increase its **PROFIT**. For example, you will often see gift vouchers in a point-of-sale display. WH Smith, for example, often displays packets of sweets at its tills, and Accessorize might display small general fashion items of small value. In all these examples, customers are likely to buy them on impulse while waiting at the till because the items are of low value.

Samples

Free samples might be offered, particularly when a new product is being launched. For example, a tasting in a supermarket, free chocolates in a specialist chocolate shop or one-use sachets of hand cream in a department store. Samples are given away so that the customer can try out the product or service and be tempted into buying it.

Free trials

Offering a free trial is a good way for a business to demonstrate how its product or service can benefit its customers before they commit to buying it. Customers are often attracted by a free trial because it gives them confidence that they do not have to spend money on the product and/or service if it is not right for them. For example, companies like Netflix and Spotify might use free trials to entice people to try their services.

Multi-buys

Supermarkets often use multi-buy promotions such as 'buy two items, get the third item free' or BOGOF ('buy one, get one free'). Superdrug and Holland & Barrett might offer the second item for 1p when the first item is purchased at full price. Promotional multi-buy offers are available across a variety of businesses throughout the year. A new and emerging business should consider whether a multi-buy offer would be the most appropriate promotional method to use if there is a large amount of competition.

Promotions can help draw customers' attention to a new product

Competitions

Competitions are a good way of promoting a business and gathering **MARKET RESEARCH** on potential customers. For example, Costa has competitions where its customers answer questions about a new product. Responders usually need to give their email address or telephone number. This then gives Costa personal information that it can store on a database and use to contact the customer. At the same time, the customer is learning about the new product and Costa is hoping that they will be tempted to purchase it.

What if...?

Shaun wants to use a promotional offer to promote his new business idea of a Pasta and Roast Meal home delivery business. The idea is to offer high quality pasta meals Monday to Saturday and a take-away roast meal on a Sunday. Shaun has the premises set up and a team in place to deliver the meals. But he is struggling to decide on the best promotional offer to use as part of his opening campaign.

1 Which type of promotional offer would you recommend to Shaun?

2 What are the reasons for your recommendation?

3 What advice or words of caution would you offer Shaun to ensure the promotion was successful?

Public relations (PR)

Any communication from a business needs to create and maintain a positive image and create a strong relationship with its audience (potential customers). This is called **PUBLIC RELATIONS (PR)**, which can take many forms. It is important that the most appropriate form is used by a business so that the communication is powerful and has a positive impact.

Press releases

Newspaper articles, or news stories, are referred to as 'editorial'. They can be used to great effect to raise the awareness or profile of a business. For example, in 2010 Mark Zuckerberg, the founder of Facebook, announced his intention to donate $100 million to schools in New Jersey, USA. This boosted the positive image of Zuckerberg's business. Other lower profile press releases can be useful to a new business, such as an article in a local paper about a business about to open, or of a business that is participating in a local charity event.

The important difference between PR and advertising is that advertising is paid for, whereas editorial coverage generated by PR is free. However, articles or news stories that result from PR campaigns are not completely within the control of the business issuing the press release. A publication may not use your press release at all or, if it does use it, your message may not come across as intended.

E-alerts

E-alerts are used by businesses to send emails to customers who have signed up to receive them. Or customers may have bought their products/services and ticked a box to agree to receiving future e-alerts. Think about your own email inbox. How many e-alerts for products and services do you receive daily, weekly or monthly?

Practise

Mark Zuckerberg announced in 2010 that he would make a multi-million donation to schools in Newark, New Jersey. He made the announcement on the *Oprah Winfrey Show* in the USA. There was speculation in the press at the time that the donation and the timing of the announcement were organised to generate positive publicity ahead of the release of the film *The Social Network*. The film was based on the life of Zuckerberg and depicted him in a way that could have led to negative publicity for his business, Facebook.

1 Do you agree with the speculation made by the press? Justify your decision.

2 What lasting impact do you think this press release had on Facebook and/or Mark Zuckerberg?

3 Can you find any recent press releases that support your argument for your answer in question 2?

Celebrity gifting and product placement

Businesses might give celebrities their products to wear or use, which the public is likely to see as an **ENDORSEMENT** (public show of approval or support) of the product. Certain products are associated with certain celebrities, and so the business must decide who the best celebrity will be to promote their business and if that celebrity is willing to wear or use the gift. For example, sports men and women might be given gadgets to use or wear – for example, a tennis player may be given a watch or a camera to use, and their fans will be more likely to buy from the same manufacturer if they want to wear or own the same **BRANDS** as their sporting idol.

Vloggers (internet video bloggers) have become celebrities in their own right through web-based channels such as YouTube. Some of the best-known vloggers have millions of subscribers. Businesses will often send a vlogger free products in the hope of a favourable mention on their YouTube channel.

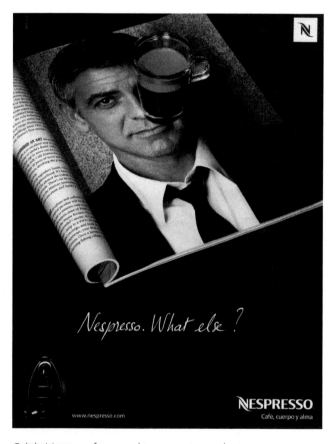

Celebrities are often used to promote products

Product placement might be everyday products strategically displayed in television programmes for the viewer to see. Businesses will pay TV programme makers to have their products used in this way. For example, a TV drama may have a branded tomato sauce placed on the table in a morning breakfast scene.

Celebrity gifting can be expensive. But product placement may be affordable to a local business if its product is needed. For example, a TV programme filmed in Cornwall may need a local product such as clotted cream.

Sponsorship

A business may decide to use part of its promotional marketing budget on **SPONSORSHIP**. The business will give money to a charity, sports team, hospital or other organisation it wants to be associated with. In return, the product or service will be promoted by the organisation. For example, football players wear the name of the team's sponsor on their shirts. This can be seen at international, national and local levels.

Hospitality

Sporting events are used by businesses to entertain their customers and promote their products or services. At most venues, there are hospitality rooms and boxes, which are areas provided free of charge to guests or visitors, where they can find a comfortable place to sit, often with free drinks. A local example would be a hospitality event at a county show or country fair. A business would hire this hospitality area during an event and use it to entertain invited guests in the hope that this might inspire loyalty among existing customers or inspire potential customers to buy from it in the future. Businesses may also invite members of the press to a hospitality event as a form of PR.

Could a hospitality opportunity be used in your local area for your own business idea?

Personal selling

A business might use people to sell its product or service to a customer face to face. There are a number of ways to do this.

- *Sales assistants in shops* are usually the first point of contact for RETAIL customers. Good customer service and product knowledge will help them to be effective in selling the products or services. For this reason, businesses need to consider the training that their sales assistants may need.
- *Pop-up stands* can be found in shopping centres or department stores and at conferences or exhibitions. Pop-up stands are temporary displays where information on products and services can be given out to potential customers or products/services purchased.
- *Door to door* – sales people can visit their potential customers' homes, usually unannounced, to promote their services and products. For example, conservatory and window businesses often use this technique.
- *Product demonstrations* are often used together with a pop-up stand, where an expert will demonstrate to the public how to use a product such as a kitchen gadget. The demonstrator will show potential customers how the product is used and will point out the benefits, such as how easy it is to operate or clean. Home demonstrations may

be more appropriate for certain products such as an expensive sound system, where the business will be keen to demonstrate exactly how its product will be of benefit in the customer's home. But unlike in-store demonstrations, home demonstrations mean that only one customer at a time can receive the demonstration.

Pop-up stands can be used to give out information to customers and to promote a business, or can be used as the back drop for a product demonstration

Direct marketing

DIRECT MARKETING (marketing material sent directly to potential customers) allows a business to personalise its communications. This can be done through a variety of media.

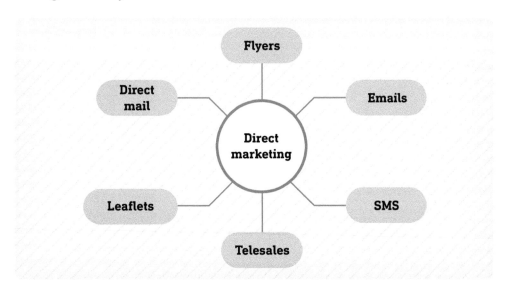

Figure 3.1: Direct marketing

Businesses need to consider many factors to make sure they are using the most appropriate direct marketing technique. They must minimise the cost of marketing, but maximise sales. Any form of communication must be clear and easy for the customer to hear or read. It should be appropriate for the product or service (for example, the right tone, 'voice' and length) and it should be timed correctly.

Table 3.3: Direct marketing techniques and factors to consider

	Emails	SMS	Direct mail	Leafleting/flyers	Telesales
What is it?	Formal and informal means of communication, which is cheap to use	Text messaging used between mobile devices	Paper-based promotional material posted directly to customers' business or home addresses	Paper-based promotional material delivered directly to customers' homes via the postal service, or inserted into newspapers/magazines. Can also be distributed by hand in store or in the street	Trained people making telephone calls to potential or existing customers to promote products or services
When would a business use it?	• To target specific people • Advertising campaigns • Newsletters	• Alternative to telephone • Reminders • Announcements	• Mail shots • Advertising campaigns • Special offers	• Mail shots • Advertising campaigns • Special offers • Discount vouchers	• Sales drive • Promote offers • Obtain information from customers
Advantages	• Message goes to identified and specific people • Can add attachments • Relatively cheap to use • Can reach all recipients in one transaction	• Can reach all recipients in one transaction • Almost instant send/receive • Will be delivered directly to recipient	• Promotional materials are delivered directly to customers' homes or businesses • Satisfies customers who prefer to read on paper	• Can be personally presented to the customer • Customer can read at their leisure • Can be kept by the customer for future reference	• Direct to the customer • Instant feedback • Telesales staff can be based anywhere
Disadvantages	• May be diverted to junk mail • Easy for potential customers to press 'delete'	• Limited information can be communicated • Number can be blocked by recipient	• Expensive • Slow • Cannot target individual customers	• Expensive • Wastage through undistributed leaflets • Can become litter	• Customer receiving unwanted calls • A need to train staff

Traditional marketing materials

In traditional marketing, printed materials might be used, usually including the business's logo.

Flyers and leaflets

Leaflets and flyers might be used by new and small businesses to promote new products or services. For example, a new gardening business might distribute flyers in the local community because local people would be its target market. Leaflets are handed out when customers ask for information and they can be kept by the customer for future reference. For example, a hairdressing business might use leaflets that give details of the different haircuts and treatments available along with a price list.

Brochures

A brochure would be used by retailers and the service industry. Brochures show pictures of products or services and describe in detail the features of each one. Brochures are used widely by car and holiday businesses that sell high-value products or services, because brochures can be expensive to produce.

Catalogues

These are usually used by retail businesses, such as clothes shops. They are designed to help the customer identify specific products or services that they want. There is usually a picture and details about each one. Argos and Ikea, for example, use catalogues. Catalogues are very expensive to produce and update, so they are usually used less often, for example by a clothing business when there is a new season.

Major retailers produce catalogues to encourage their customers to browse the products offered at their leisure. Flyers and leaflets are used by a variety of businesses to give specific information on their products or services. Tour operators use brochures to promote holiday destinations

Posters

Posters are displayed in many places and in many sizes. They are designed to attract attention. You might see them at bus stops, on billboards, inside public transport and in shop windows.

Business cards

A business card contains written information about the business, usually address and contact details. It will remind customers how to contact the business in the future. The design of a business card is important because this will convey the brand image of the business.

Practise

Do some research into the businesses in your area that use traditional methods of marketing. Answer the following questions:

1 What is the most common traditional method used by these businesses?

2 What is the promotional message being conveyed by the businesses, and what is the likely impact on its customers?

3 Which traditional methods would work for your own enterprise idea? Explain your answer.

A2 Strengths and weaknesses of different promotional methods in relation to the enterprise idea

Each different promotional method has its own strengths and weaknesses. It is important that you can identify these so that you select the most appropriate method to help your enterprise idea succeed.

Reaching the target market

The promotional method you use must be aimed at your target market. Your business could waste much time and money if your promotional materials are seen or heard only by people who are unlikely to buy your products or services.

Supporting sales

When a promotion is successful and sales are made, the business must be able to cope with the increased activity and the associated increase in workload. For example, if a product becomes very popular because of a recent promotional campaign, the business must make sure that it has plenty of the products in stock and staff available to meet the increased demand. So the business needs to calculate the likely increase in sales that each different promotional method might lead to.

Increasing sales volume

Promotional methods must increase the chances of people buying the product or service. If a promotional method does not give enough information for a customer to make a decision, or there is so much information that the customer is overwhelmed, the customer is unlikely to buy it.

The type of information a customer needs might include specific details about what the product or service does, the different models or colours available and how to make a purchase. For example, if a promotional leaflet does not give a full explanation of what a product or service is capable of, potential customers will not know its features or benefits and are less likely to want to buy it. Likewise, if telephone numbers or email addresses are left out of promotional materials, customers might not know how to obtain the product or service.

Drawing up a list of strengths and weaknesses can help you to decide which promotional methods to use

Suitability for the customer base

Each target market will have a unique profile and specific needs. So the promotional methods you use must match the needs and expectations of your **CUSTOMER BASE** (the type of people your customers are). For example, a children's clothing business may decide to purchase a customer database of young families to send a series of emails to promote a new range of upmarket children's clothing.

It is important that this database contains the names and email addresses of individuals who would be interested in these products, for example, young families who are able to afford them. So more information, such as the spending habits and incomes of those on the database, would need to be considered to make sure that only those who can afford the products are targeted.

Affordability

All promotional methods will come with a cost. So the business needs to consider how much of its budget to allocate to promotions and how it can maximise the available budget so that the promotional methods it uses are the most effective for the budget available.

Expensive promotional methods such as TV advertising might be appropriate if national coverage is required to reach many different types of potential customers. TV advertisements are eye-catching and can give very specific information. On the other hand, cheaper methods of promotion such as an email campaign would be more appropriate for a business that only wants to target specific individuals.

Supporting the brand

Consideration needs to be given to the way promotional materials are produced and used and how this fits in with the business's brand. For example, an expensive sound system might be promoted using high-quality paper to convey the idea that the product being promoted is good quality. On the other hand, organic products promoted on recycled paper will show the customer that the business cares about the environment. In both these examples, the promotional methods are promoting values that the business wants customers to associate with the brand.

Skills and knowledge check

- [ ] Describe the benefits of using direct mail.
- [ ] List three important factors that a business should consider when choosing a direct marketing technique.
- [ ] Give an example of a business that uses each of the five direct marketing techniques in Table 3.3.
- [ ] Give two examples of different promotional methods and explain who the target market is likely to be for each example.

- ○ I can explain the differences between each of the promotional methods.
- ○ I can describe each of the five PR techniques that can be used to promote products or services.
- ○ I have thought about and can describe which promotional method would be most suitable for my own enterprise idea.

B Produce a promotional plan for the enterprise idea

In this section, you will produce a **PROMOTIONAL PLAN** for your enterprise idea. A promotional plan outlines the way in which a business will raise awareness of its product or service.

B1 Developing an idea for test/field marketing

When a new business is starting, it is important to test the target market to see what customers think about the product or service.

Test marketing plan

Do customers like the product/service? Do they feel it would be useful to them? How often are they likely to use it? This is all useful information to a new business. A plan should be made of the test, also known as field, marketing that the business will do. Here are a few examples.

a   Identify a small subset of the market – a target market can be broken down into smaller target markets, or subsets, each with specific characteristics (such as age). The enterprise idea can then be tested on the different subsets to find out who is most likely to buy the product or service so that, when the full marketing campaign is launched, it will target the most appropriate part of the market.

b   Identify a representative **SAMPLE** size – a large sample (the people you ask to participate in your research) will bring in more responses and is more likely to provide accurate findings than a small sample. But if you

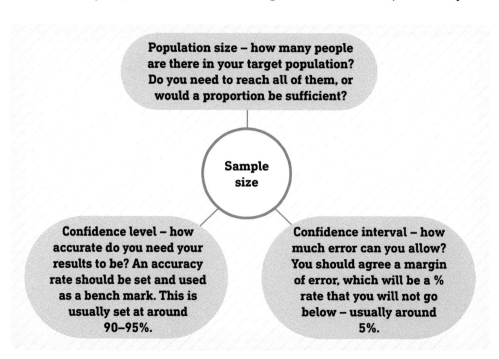

Figure 3.2: Identifying a representative sample size

use a large sample, you could be swamped with responses that will be time consuming to go through.

c   Establish an appropriate method for the test – the most widely used methods to test markets are **QUESTIONNAIRES**, surveys and product sampling. But the type of method will affect the results. For example, if you ask questions about an enterprise idea, the respondent is likely to give a different answer than they would if you first let them experience the product or service itself.

d   Assess the **VALIDITY** and reliability of findings – validity is when the results of any test or survey are factually accurate and logical. Reliability is when the results of any test or survey will give the same results when repeated. When you have gathered your findings from your test sampling, you need to consider their validity and reliability. For example, if you have not made sure that your findings truly represent the target market, they will not be reliable. If the questions on a questionnaire lead the respondent into giving a particular answer, the results will not be valid.

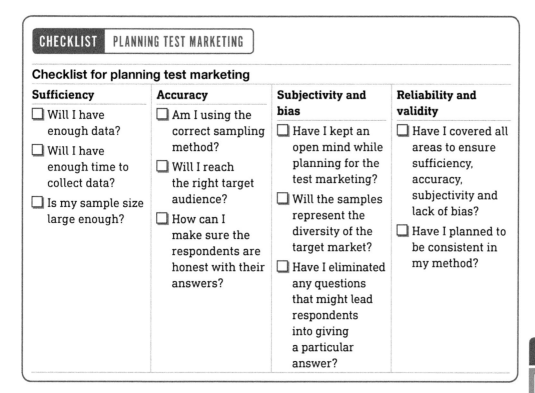

CHECKLIST | **PLANNING TEST MARKETING**

Checklist for planning test marketing

Sufficiency	Accuracy	Subjectivity and bias	Reliability and validity
☐ Will I have enough data? ☐ Will I have enough time to collect data? ☐ Is my sample size large enough?	☐ Am I using the correct sampling method? ☐ Will I reach the right target audience? ☐ How can I make sure the respondents are honest with their answers?	☐ Have I kept an open mind while planning for the test marketing? ☐ Will the samples represent the diversity of the target market? ☐ Have I eliminated any questions that might lead respondents into giving a particular answer?	☐ Have I covered all areas to ensure sufficiency, accuracy, subjectivity and lack of bias? ☐ Have I planned to be consistent in my method?

e   Draw conclusions to inform promotion and planning – you will need to plan how you will pull together all the information from the test marketing. Look back to the main purpose of your marketing and the marketing objectives that you set to achieve your desired outcomes – are these being achieved?

B2 Developing strategies for the promotional campaign

You can use a number of marketing tools in your marketing plan to come up with an overall strategy. You may want to use a variety of marketing tools that share the same message and ideas to reinforce it to your customers for maximum impact. Table 3.4 explores why this would be a good strategy.

Link it up

Unit 2, learning aim C, looks at market research, and the methods commonly used to carry it out, in more depth.

Table 3.4: Using a variety of marketing tools

What would be the benefit?	Why do it?
Raise awareness of new or existing products or services	If customers are not aware of any new or existing products or services, they will not be able to buy them. So it is vital that the business gives its products or services maximum exposure through more than one type of marketing tool or method.
Remind customers about existing products or services	For larger, or one-off, purchases, a customer is likely to read about the product or service at least six times before they make a purchase. So an important marketing strategy is to build 'reminder' messages into your plan.
Demonstrate how the product or service differs from that offered by competitors	There is so much competition in most markets that a business must consider how to make sure its promotions will make its products or services the first choice for potential customers.
Inform customers about the features of the product or service	Highlighting the features of your products or services is important because customers will want to know details like what a product is made of, the colours available and its size. The marketing tools you use must clearly outline the key features that will be of most interest to the target audience. A good way to choose which features to include in your marketing materials is to think of how each feature will benefit the customer.
Persuade customers of the benefits of purchasing the product or service	A customer is more likely to purchase what you are selling if they can see how they will benefit from it. So your marketing tools must be clear in how they set out the benefits to the target audience, with clear links to the features of the product or service.
Create market presence by delivering a clear message about the product or service	Presence in a market is key to a successful business. This is most often done by establishing a good brand image, for example through the business's name or logo. If a customer wanting to purchase a certain product or service immediately thinks of your business, you know that your marketing campaign has been successful.

Link it up

Unit 2, learning aim C, looks at marketing tools in relation to the marketing mix.

Creating a market presence: one of the office products in this picture is immediately associated with a well-known brand name in most people's minds

Practise

Think about why you would want to use a variety of marketing tools when promoting your own enterprise idea. Answer the following questions.

1 Which promotional methods would be most effective in maximising sales of your products or services to your target market? Give reasons for your answer.

2 What techniques could you use as a 'follow up' to remind your customers?

3 What are the features and benefits of your product or service? What are the key messages that you need to consider putting onto your promotional materials?

B3 Planning a costed promotional campaign

SMART promotional objectives

Using **SMART** (specific, measurable, achievable, realistic, time-bound) objectives is key to ensuring that your promotional campaign stays focused. The objectives should be a part of the planning process. To set objectives, you need to think about what you want to achieve from your marketing campaign, which may be financial, non-financial or a combination of both.

Figure 3.3: SMART promotional objectives

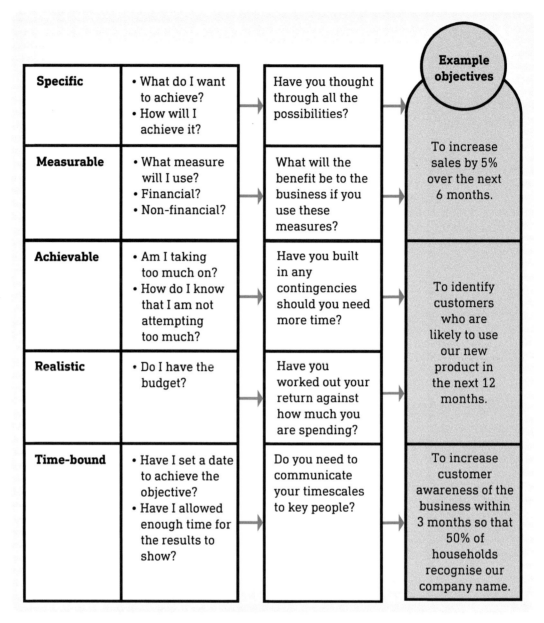

Figure 3.4: Example of SMART objectives

Practise

Think about what you want to achieve within your promotional campaign, how you will measure your success and the timescale for the promotion and its success. Write at least three objectives for your own enterprise idea.

Link it up

You will use SMART objectives for more business targets in Unit 4 (B1) when you present your business plan.

Selecting the most appropriate methods and materials

Different promotional methods and different marketing materials will bring different results. Any promotion will cost money, time and effort, so it is essential that you choose the most appropriate promotional method and marketing materials to increase the likelihood that your enterprise idea will be a success.

Campaign objectives

By using SMART promotional objectives, you can focus on what is important to you and your enterprise idea and what you need to do to achieve a good outcome. It will help you, and anyone else involved in your promotional campaign, to stay focused, because you can return to the objectives on a regular basis to ensure that your campaign is on track.

Suitability

Not all promotional methods and marketing materials will be suitable or appropriate for your enterprise idea. You need to choose the method that will reflect the brand image of your business and communicate this to your customers in a medium that will reach them. For example, an email or SMS promotional campaign will only be successful if the target market has the ability to receive emails or text messages. On the other hand, leaflets will only work if customers have the time to read them.

Audience

It is important to keep in mind your target market, which is also your audience. Have you created marketing materials that will appeal to them? Does it reflect their lifestyle? Are you using language that they can identify with?

Budget

The amount of money you spend on your promotional campaign can contribute to its success or failure. If you spend too much and go above your budget, there will be no benefit to your business – your profits will be swallowed up by your over-spend. Likewise, if you stay well under budget, you may not reach a wider audience and so you will not maximise your opportunities for sales.

Skills and knowledge check

- [ ] Why set SMART objectives for your promotional campaign?
- [ ] Why is it important to be aware of your audience when deciding on the most appropriate promotional methods and marketing materials to use?
- [ ] What could happen if you go over your budget?
- [ ] Name the three key factors to consider when deciding on your sample size for testing the market.

- ○ I can explain what each letter stands for in 'SMART'.
- ○ I have written down promotional objectives for my enterprise idea that are SMART.
- ○ I can describe three benefits of using marketing tools to support my marketing strategy.

C Produce a financial plan for the enterprise idea

In this section, you will produce a **FINANCIAL PLAN** for your enterprise idea, which details how you will pay for your business activities.

C1 Financial plan

A plan of how you will spend the money to finance your enterprise idea and where it will come from will ensure that you have enough funds to get you to the start-up point and beyond. You will be able to work out what your costs are likely to be and identify the point at which you will start making a profit. You need to be able to project your costs beyond start-up and identify how your **INCOME** will be generated and what you expect your revenue to be (the money a business makes from sales).

Classifying fixed and variable costs

Link it up

For more on fixed and variable costs, look back at Table 1.16 in Unit 1.

Your enterprise business idea will have **FIXED COSTS** and **VARIABLE COSTS**. Fixed costs are costs that will not change, but are necessary for the business to run. Variable costs are costs that will vary according to the business activity, so as the business becomes busier, these costs are likely to go up. A business must know its fixed and variable costs so that it can control them, and, where possible, make changes to reduce the costs. It will also help the business to know how much revenue it needs so that all of its costs are covered.

Table 3.5: Examples of fixed and variable costs

Fixed costs	Variable costs
Rent	Products to sell
Council tax	Materials to make products or provide a service
Insurance	Laundry costs
Telephone line rental	Telephone calls

The break-even point

A **BREAK-EVEN POINT** for a business is when the total **REVENUE** equals the total costs. This means that the money being received from sales is the same as the money being spent on costs. When the break-even point has been reached, the business is then likely to start making a profit. So, if a business can forecast its break-even point, for example on a monthly basis, it will give a good indication of when all costs have been covered and the business will start to make a profit. In some cases, the break-even forecast might be given over a yearly forecast. A business must be able to calculate its break-even point and then interpret the figures within it.

The break-even point can be calculated using the formula below:

$$\text{Break-even point} = \frac{\text{fixed costs}}{\text{Selling price} - \text{variable costs per unit}}$$

Selling price – variable costs per unit is called 'the contribution per unit'. So

$$\text{Break-even point} = \frac{\text{fixed costs}}{\text{Contribution per unit}}$$

For example:

(Worked example 1)

Fay makes celebration cakes from a rented kitchen. She has fixed costs of £20,000. Her variable cost per cake is £10 and her selling price is £26.

contribution per unit = 26 – 10 = 16

$$\text{break-even point} = \frac{\text{fixed costs}}{\text{contribution per unit}}$$

$$\text{break-even point} = \frac{£20,000}{£16} = 1\,250 \text{ cakes}$$

Fay must sell 1 250 cakes to achieve break-even. If she sells fewer than this she will make a loss. If she sells more she will make a profit.

If Fay sells 1 251 cakes she will make £16 profit, because after break-even has been reached, the contribution per unit no longer has to contribute towards fixed costs and therefore becomes profit.

How much profit would Fay make if she sold 1 500 cakes?

(Worked Example 2)

Assume Fay sold 1 500 cakes.

margin of safety
= actual sale in units – break-even level of output

margin of safety
= 1 500 cakes – 1 250 cakes = 250 cakes

Figure 3.5: Fixed and variable costs

Appropriate sources of finance for the financial plan

A business needs to consider how it will be financed, and this could be for long and short periods of time. Short term is usually up to six months and long term from six months onwards. How the business intends to use the finance and for what purpose will usually determine if a short or long-term solution is required.

Link it up

Look back at Unit 1 (D3) to remind yourself how to calculate the break-even point.

Table 3.6: Examples of short-term sources of finance

Type of short-term finance	Benefits	Points to consider	Costs involved
Supplier credit	Usually there is no cost to this type of finance.	It is only a short-term solution, and charges may be applied if you do not pay by the agreed date. Credit terms are stated within the terms and conditions of the credit agreement.	As long as the business keeps to the terms and conditions of the credit agreement, there is usually no cost.
Bank overdraft	The overdraft can be paid off when there are funds available without any penalties.	The rate of interest is high and the bank can request the overdraft be paid back at any time and even without notice. When the business has used all of its overdraft, the bank may refuse to lend any more money, or may agree a larger overdraft. The business needs to consider, if more money is borrowed short-term, how it will be able to pay the bank back.	The bank will most likely charge a setting-up fee of £100 or more, and interest rates tend to be high.

Table 3.7: Examples of long-term sources of finance

Type of long-term finance	Benefits	Points to consider	Costs involved
Bank loan	The length of time for the loan is agreed between the business and the bank. The business can then budget the monthly payment, which stays the same throughout the length of the loan.	The interest charged for the loan is usually added at the beginning of the loan. The first few months or years of payments (depending on the length of the loan) are usually just paying off the interest. Banks will calculate an early settlement figure which the business can accept, or it can continue to repay the loan.	Interest will be charged and there may be a set-up cost for a business loan.
Personal savings	The money is available immediately, and there are no charges.	Personal savings could be used as a 'safety net' for a business, so when these are used up, the business loses this security. If personal savings are invested wisely in a high-interest account, they may earn enough interest to offset some of the charges of a bank loan.	Any potential interest the personal savings may have earned if it had been invested in a high-interest account.
Retained profit	The business can benefit from the profits it has made.	All costs and outstanding debts should be paid in full to calculate the retained profit. Retained profit could be kept to give the business financial security for emergencies.	None, other than any potential interest the retained profit may have earned if it had been invested in a high-interest account.

What if...?

Yasmine is a trained florist and has decided to open a stall in her local market three days a week. She will be selling flowers and taking orders for flower arrangements for special occasions. On the days that she is not on her stall, she plans to make up the flower arrangement orders that she hopes to take. Yasmine needs to raise £500 to paint the market stall and purchase containers to display her flowers in. Yasmine has savings of £250 and is not sure whether to use her savings and get a loan for the rest, or to get a loan for the entire £500.

1 What type of loan would you recommend that Yasmine considers? Give reasons for your answer.

2 What length of time would you recommend Yasmine has her loan over? Give reasons for your answer

3 Do some internet research to find out how much this loan is likely to cost.

Link it up

Look back at Unit 1 (D3) if you need to remind yourself of the importance of cash-flow forecasting and how to complete a forecast from given information.

Cash-flow forecast

When forecasting cash flow (the amount of money coming in and out), a business must be realistic about the amount of sales it will make. It must take into account busy and quiet periods, where sales will increase or decrease. It must also be prepared for any expected costs, such as equipment replacement, as well as having a contingency for unexpected costs, for example when equipment breaks down.

Seasons and public holidays should be factored in, particularly public holidays where the business may close or customers may be less likely to make purchases. Builders' merchants, for example, must consider when their customers, who are builders, will also be on holiday, and so cash flow will be reduced. Other businesses will be open on public holidays to maximise sales opportunities, such as retailers and cafés, so increasing their cash flow. This should be factored in against the costs, which may not be seasonal, such as fixed costs.

The revenue, or income received by the business

The total amount of income received each month is calculated

All the money that a business has to pay out

One-off costs at start-up will have an impact on how much money is in the bank

The total amount of income spent each month is calculated

As the sales income increases, so do these variable costs

Fixed costs so stay the same each month

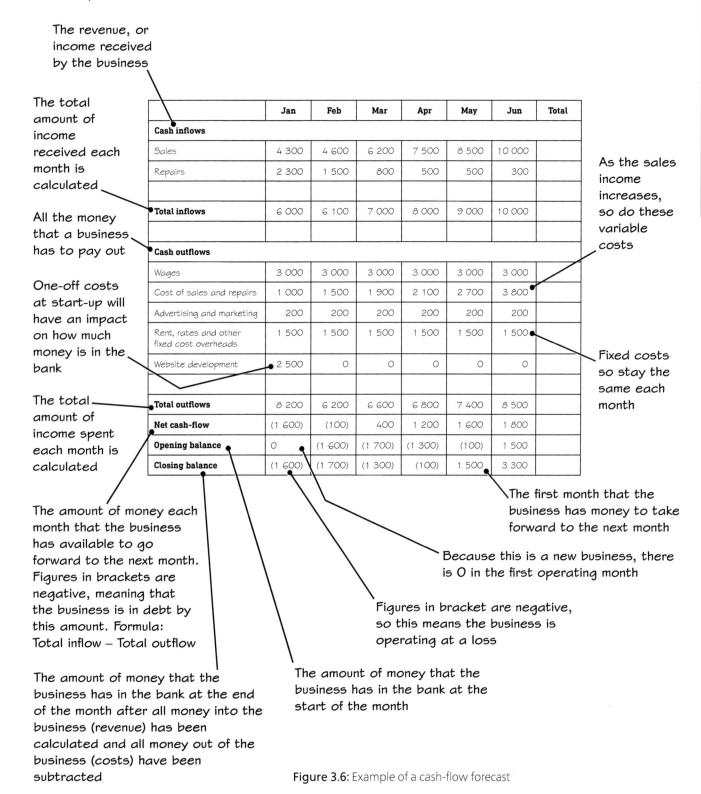

	Jan	Feb	Mar	Apr	May	Jun	Total
Cash inflows							
Sales	4 300	4 600	6 200	7 500	8 500	10 000	
Repairs	2 300	1 500	800	500	500	300	
Total inflows	6 000	6 100	7 000	8 000	9 000	10 000	
Cash outflows							
Wages	3 000	3 000	3 000	3 000	3 000	3 000	
Cost of sales and repairs	1 000	1 500	1 900	2 100	2 700	3 800	
Advertising and marketing	200	200	200	200	200	200	
Rent, rates and other fixed cost overheads	1 500	1 500	1 500	1 500	1 500	1 500	
Website development	2 500	0	0	0	0	0	
Total outflows	8 200	6 200	6 600	6 800	7 400	8 500	
Net cash-flow	(1 600)	(100)	400	1 200	1 600	1 800	
Opening balance	0	(1 600)	(1 700)	(1 300)	(100)	1 500	
Closing balance	(1 600)	(1 700)	(1 300)	(100)	1 500	3 300	

The amount of money each month that the business has available to go forward to the next month. Figures in brackets are negative, meaning that the business is in debt by this amount. Formula: Total inflow – Total outflow

The amount of money that the business has in the bank at the end of the month after all money into the business (revenue) has been calculated and all money out of the business (costs) have been subtracted

The amount of money that the business has in the bank at the start of the month

Figures in bracket are negative, so this means the business is operating at a loss

Because this is a new business, there is 0 in the first operating month

The first month that the business has money to take forward to the next month

Figure 3.6: Example of a cash-flow forecast

The predicted income statement (profit and loss account)

It is important that a business predicts on a monthly basis how much income it expects to receive and how much it will spend as the business needs to know if it can cover its costs. The **CASH-FLOW FORECAST** can be the basis for the predicted **INCOME STATEMENT** (a document reporting the income generated by a business in a particular period of time, also called the profit and loss account). From the predicted income statement the business can determine when less income is coming into the business so that it can avoid large purchases. When a new business starts up there will be costs that cannot be avoided and so the business needs to ensure there is sufficient finance to cover any debt while the business becomes established.

An income statement will list all the revenue a business has received and all its costs. The costs are taken away from the revenue, and the result will be the amount of profit or loss for the period that is being accounted for.

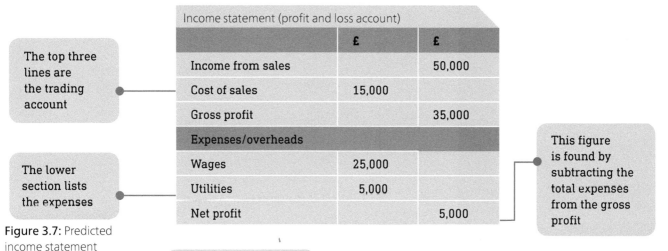

The top three lines are the trading account

The lower section lists the expenses

Income statement (profit and loss account)		
	£	£
Income from sales		50,000
Cost of sales	15,000	
Gross profit		35,000
Expenses/overheads		
Wages	25,000	
Utilities	5,000	
Net profit		5,000

This figure is found by subtracting the total expenses from the gross profit

Figure 3.7: Predicted income statement

Costs of promotion

The financial plan must clearly show and detail all the costs for promoting and marketing the new business. This will ensure that the promotions used are appropriate for the business in terms of cost against predicted income and predicted sales. Costs of promotion should be shown under the expenses/overheads section of an income statement.

Estimating viability and contributing factors as situations change

Not all costs will be known to a new business and so there will be an element of guess work, where the business will have to estimate its anticipated costs. These should be monitored and updated as costs become known, or as soon as the business sees that these have been under or over-estimated.

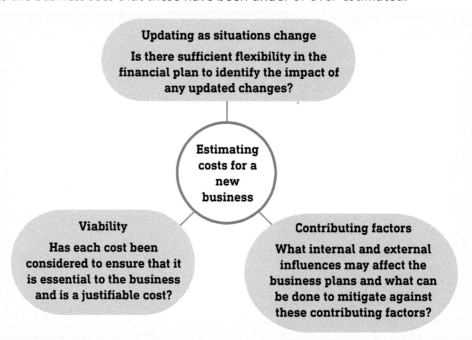

Updating as situations change

Is there sufficient flexibility in the financial plan to identify the impact of any updated changes?

Estimating costs for a new business

Viability

Has each cost been considered to ensure that it is essential to the business and is a justifiable cost?

Contributing factors

What internal and external influences may affect the business plans and what can be done to mitigate against these contributing factors?

Figure 3.8: Estimating costs for a new business

Timescales and financial commitments

A financial plan must be written to meet the requirements of the timescales of the overall business plan. For example, the business premises will need to be financed in advance of any stock or displays being ordered, and all of this must fit into the plan for when the business will be open to its customers.

Short-term timescales might be 6 months. Long-term timescales might be 2 years.

> ### Practise
>
> Create a cash-flow forecast for your own enterprise idea. Think about how the business will receive money, and make a list of these revenue streams. List all the fixed and variable costs that the business will have to bear. Calculate how much revenue and the costs to the business you expect for each month, and write this into your forecast.
>
> 1 Which months will bring in the most revenue?
>
> 2 Which months will have the most costs?
>
> 3 When will the business start to make money?

C2 The supply chain for the enterprise idea

The supply chain

The **SUPPLY CHAIN** is a sequence of events or processes that a business will set up and use to source materials or stock that it will manufacture or sell to the customer. There are four basic steps that a business must follow.

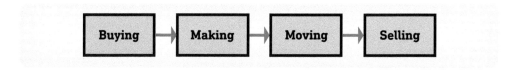

Figure 3.9: The supply chain

Buying

Whether a business is manufacturing products, buying in components to assemble, or purchasing stock to sell on or use as part of any services it is selling, it must decide where to purchase what it needs. The business must consider where it can get the best value for money and which suppliers will be reliable and give it the best terms, such as credit arrangements or discounts.

Making

The next stage for a manufacturing business is to consider whether it will make the products to sell on, use a third party or do a combination of these.

Moving

When the products are made and ready to be sold, they need to reach the customers. This part of the supply chain involves logistics. Logistics is the transportation of products from the supplier to the customer. Large businesses are likely to use a logistics company to get their products to the shops to be sold. For example, Stobart Group carries products for a wide range of businesses from supermarkets to engineering companies. You can regularly see an Eddie Stobart lorry on the motorway.

Smaller businesses may distribute their own products because they would not be able to afford the services of a large logistics company. For example, a small picture framing company in Somerset might make its own picture frames and deliver them to its customers once a week using its own company van.

Selling

The final part of the supply chain is how and where the products or services will be sold. Many different outlets can be used, and businesses will often use more than one type. The business must decide where its customers are most likely to purchase its products or services – for example, online, out of town supermarkets, high street shops, market stalls, seasonal roadside outlets or via telesales.

For example, Screwfix sells its building and DIY products through physical shops, online and by telephone – whereas a small craft business is likely to sell its products on a market stall or at craft fairs.

A small stall will have fewer overheads than a shop, though a city-centre pitch could still be quite expensive

Factors to consider in an effective supply chain

An efficient supply chain will make sure that the business can meet the demands of its customers and do so on time. The stages of the supply chain vary according to the product or service, and the following need to be considered.

Quality of source

Buying the cheapest materials or products to sell on is not necessarily a wise choice. If the materials are not fit for purpose or are poor quality, the finished product will be inferior. Customer expectations will then not be met, which will lead to customer complaints, resulting in damage to the business's reputation and the potential loss of customers.

Accessibility

The business needs to consider the diversity of its customer base and whether all customers will have access to its products and/or services. For example, if a business chooses to sell its products or services in a bricks-and-mortar shop (as opposed to an online shop), there must be easy access for pushchairs and wheelchair users.

Prices

Value for money means ensuring that the best quality products or materials are purchased at the best possible price. If the business purchases raw materials or products at the wrong price, it can result in loss of profits. For example, an outside burger bar advertising 'gourmet' style beef burgers and selling them at a premium price must make the burgers using high-quality steak so that customer expectations are met.

If the burger company was to make its burgers with low-quality meat, the customers might complain and not purchase the burgers again, so that the burger company will not be successful. On the other hand, a fast food burger company selling its burgers at competitive prices, but using high-quality steak for ingredients, may find that it cannot cover its costs because customers do not expect to pay a higher price for these burgers.

Workable cash flow

A **WORKABLE CASH FLOW** means having enough money available to cover the day-to-day running of the business, such as wages, paying suppliers and other low-cost consumables such as stationery, postage and fuel for vehicles. Without a workable cash flow, a business is unable to function and will quickly lose the ability to meet the needs of its customers. For example, if a café owner cannot pay its food suppliers, they will stop delivering the food and the café will have no meals to serve to its customers.

Businesses need to have money to cover day-to-day expenses, like fuel for vehicles

Service and support for customers

The business needs to consider how the supply chain might affect its customer service. For example, if a business uses a supplier that offers a guarantee on the materials or products it supplies, the business will be able to pass this guarantee onto customers. This will build customer confidence and satisfaction. **AFTERSALES SERVICE** is also important, so using suppliers who can offer support to the business will increase the amount of support the business can offer its customers. This might include supplying spare parts or repairs for products sold.

Quantities

Minimum and maximum ordering capacity is important. For example, a supplier may have a minimum order size, but the business needs to ensure that it does not over-order and end up with vast quantities of materials or products that it will not be able to use or sell. On the other hand, suppliers need to be able to guarantee that they can consistently supply and maintain repeat orders to a business for customers who want to regularly purchase the same products.

Think of supermarkets and corner shops. They sell regular food products from major suppliers such as Heinz, Branston and Kingsmill. They need to ensure that they are able to get a regular supply of the correct quantities so that they can meet their customers' demands. Likewise, Heinz, Branston and Kingsmill need to obtain the ingredients to make their products from reliable suppliers who can supply the vast quantities required to meet the national demand.

Delivery arrangements

Delivery arrangements are important to ensure that the business receives its products or materials at an appropriate time to be able to function. For example, a shop selling newspapers will want them delivered early in the morning so that the newspapers can be prepared for a newspaper delivery round before the shop opens and before the paper deliverer arrives. On the other hand, large or high-value items such as electrical products cannot be delivered to a shop until the shop is open and a staff member is present to receive them.

Relationship with suppliers

Building a good relationship with the supplier will help the reliability of supplies. It is important that products and materials arrive on time and are available when ordered. The business owner can help to ensure a good relationship with the supplier by paying their bills on time, ordering what they require in good time and being available to receive deliveries.

Credit terms

A supplier will usually offer credit terms to the business where a maximum amount of money is agreed that the business can owe for products, materials and/or ingredients that it has purchased. This debt must then be paid within an agreed timescale, usually 30 or 60 days. If the business does not pay its supplier within the agreed timescales, the supplier may charge interest on the outstanding amount. When the business has reached its credit limit, the supplier might refuse to offer any more credit until the amount owed is paid, and any orders until then will have to be paid for in full at the time of purchase.

Ethical considerations

CARBON EMISSIONS (harmful carbon dioxide emissions) are an issue for some businesses, for example shops that sell local produce. These businesses will often promote the fact that they are offering locally sourced products as part of their **UNIQUE SELLING POINT**, or USP. For example they might work with local suppliers to keep their **CARBON FOOTPRINT** (the amount of carbon dioxide produced by a business) to a minimum. Another environmental consideration is **SUSTAINABILITY** (where a business offsets any environmental damage it causes). When natural resources, such as wood, are involved – this would entail buying timber through schemes that ensure trees are replanted.

Another example of a USP is Fair Trade, where people employed within the supply chain – for example Asian textile workers – receive fair pay for their products.

Purchasing process

The process of purchasing products/materials has a number of steps.

	How the purchasing process works
Order	The business places an order for products, materials or ingredients that includes item description, or identification number such as a part number, and quantity.
Delivery	• Choices include delivery or collection. • Delivery may include a charge, which will be confirmed at the time of order. • Any special delivery instructions should be given, e.g. cash on delivery or where to leave items.
LEAD TIME	• This is how long it will take for the items to be delivered when the order has been made. • The business should pay particular attention to the lead time to ensure stocks do not run out and to manage the expectation of the customer for one-off personalised orders.
Payment	• If there is a credit agreement, the business will receive an invoice that will list the items purchased and the price of each item. • If there is no credit arrangement, the business will be expected to pay for items that it purchases and receives. • Cash on delivery may be offered when items are delivered to the business.

Table 3.8: The purchasing process

Practise

Think about the supply chain for your own enterprise idea and answer the following questions:

1 Will your business make, manufacture or just supply products or services?

2 Who will your suppliers be?

3 How will you get your products or services to the locations where you will sell them?

4 Where will you sell your products or services?

5 What main considerations will you need to make with regard to your supply chain process?

Skills and knowledge check

- ☐ What is revenue?
- ☐ What is an opening balance?
- ☐ What is a closing balance?
- ☐ Explain the difference between variable and fixed costs.
- ☐ What does it mean when a figure is in brackets?

- ◯ I can calculate the break-even point for my enterprise.
- ◯ I understand the different sources of finance available to me and the factors I need to consider.
- ◯ I can complete a cash-flow forecast for my enterprise.
- ◯ I can describe the supply chain from the start to the end.

Ready for assessment

You will be assessed for this unit through two practical tasks.

1 In the first task, you will create a promotional plan for a promotional campaign for your enterprise idea that includes SMART objectives. This will be based on a product or service that you want to promote in a specific business, and you will need to justify your choice of promotional methods that you have outlined in your plan.

2 In the second task, you will create a financial plan for your enterprise idea.

You will need to show that you have researched a number of promotional methods, including digital and online media resources as well as traditional methods, and that you have identified the strengths and weaknesses of each method. You should show that you have thought through the links between the promotional methods you intend to use and the SMART objectives that you set for the promotion of your enterprise idea, giving reasons for your choice of promotional methods and how you will meet the timescales of your promotion.

Any promotional methods that you intend to use that are in your plan should be appropriate to your target market, and you should explain how you have taken this into consideration as part of the planning process. You should explain why the methods you have chosen are appropriate to your target market, and why those that you have not chosen are not.

You should detail your plans for test, or field, marketing, and test out an element of your promotional plan where additional refinement would be beneficial to its success. The test plan should contain specified objectives and an indication of how your conclusions will inform your on-going plans.

You should retain any research notes that you undertake and keep records of websites that you visit. Practical evidence could include:

- leaflets, flyers or any other promotional materials you produce

- emails and/or SMS messages you create as part of your promotional campaign

- test marketing plan and any practical research activities attached to this

- tables showing different types of business loans or finance options with costs

- list of suppliers appropriate to your business

- supply-chain option flow charts

- cash-flow forecasts

- any calculations of costs

- promotional plan

- financial plan

- notes from employer visits.

You should keep original versions of any updated calculations, such as your cash-flow forecast or first draft of promotional plans, test marketing plans and financial plans to demonstrate how you have improved and refined your enterprise idea.

WORK FOCUS

HANDS ON

You will practise important skills throughout this unit to demonstrate your entrepreneurial aptitude and commercial acumen, both of which are essential for an enterprise idea to be transformed into a successful business.

It is important that you know and understand the important factors that make a business successful, including:

- financial planning
- knowing how to interpret financial statements, including cash-flow statements
- the importance of the supply chain, the key processes and what makes these effective
- the variety of promotional methods available and which methods should be used with which target market
- the components of a promotional plan
- how to create an effective promotional plan.

Do:

- research: it is important that you know what is available to you, whether it is finance options or what products are popular with your target market
- have your finances in place: if you do not have enough funds and you run out of money, your business will not succeed
- work out your supply chain
- plan for the unexpected and have contingencies in all your planning.

Don't:

- leave things to chance – if you ignore a hunch, you may live to regret it
- over spend: prioritise between what is essential for the business and what would be 'nice to have', even when planning
- ignore test planning: a test plan will give you vital information that may lead to you changing the way you do things.

Work experience

Use your work experience to test out your ideas by talking to other people in your work placement. Ask them what they think about different promotional methods and why they think that some work and others do not. Create a questionnaire to take with you to your work placement that will help you when creating your own promotional plan. Example questions could include:

- What promotional methods does the work placement use?
- How do these methods relate to their target market?
- How effective are they?
- What is the supply chain process?
- How many suppliers do they use?
- What are the delivery arrangements?

What other questions could you ask?

Ready for work?

Match up the correct sentences:

A When deciding on an appropriate promotional method, you should	**1** help the business with its cash flow
B SMART objectives should be used to	**2** consider the target market
C Arranging credit terms will	**3** help to ensure products are always in stock
D A cash-flow forecast will	**4** help the business focus on its goals
E Knowing the lead time within the supply chain will	**5** identify revenue and costs per month to aid planning

Were there any sentences you struggled to match up correctly? If yes, then go back to the relevant learning aims in this unit to refresh your memory.

4 Planning and Pitching an Enterprise Idea

Do you want to be the next Richard Branson? Do you have an idea for a new product or service that you think could develop into a viable business venture?

In this unit you will have the opportunity to bring together all your ideas from the previous units and plan in more detail. You will then 'pitch' your idea to a range of individuals, including employers, advisers and investors, to gain financial backing to take your new business idea forward.

How will I be assessed?

You will have the opportunity to work with industry mentors, employers and others to develop a business plan based on a new or existing idea. You will need to produce the business plan in a professional, structured format. The plan will include all of the relevant details, including an analysis of risks.

When the business plan is presented for assessment, you will then PITCH your idea using all the relevant data and product information. To pitch your idea means to present it to an audience. Your presentation will be observed and may be recorded. The audience for the presentation pitch may vary, but could include employers, advisers and potential investors. Following the pitch, you will be asked to analyse your pitch and presentation skills based on feedback from everyone involved. The results of the analysis will form the basis for a set of recommendations to take your idea forward.

Assessment criteria

Pass	Merit	Distinction
Learning aim A: Prepare a business plan for the new enterprise idea		
A.P1 Produce a structured business plan for an enterprise idea that includes key risks.	**A.M1** Produce a structured and integrated business plan for an enterprise idea that includes a description of risks.	**A.D1** Produce a structured, integrated and detailed business plan for an enterprise idea that includes an analysis of risks.
Learning aim B: Present a business pitch to an audience including a potential investor or business adviser		
B.P2 Prepare a business pitch for the business plan supported by relevant business documents.	**B.M2** Deliver a clear and structured pitch for the business plan, responding to audience questions appropriately.	**B.D2** Deliver a confident and well-structured pitch for the business plan, exploring aspects that are questioned with the audience.
B.P3 Deliver a clear pitch for the business plan to a potential sponsor that contains key features.		
Learning aim C: Review and revise the business plan to respond to feedback		
C.P4 Use pitch feedback to make changes to the business plan.	**C.M3** Reflect on pitch feedback, and own performance, to explain improvements to the business plan.	**C.D3** Analyse the business plan and enterprise idea based on pitch feedback and own performance, and justify a set of recommendations.

A Prepare a business plan for the new enterprise idea

A business plan is a working document that can help you to develop your ideas. It will help you to work through some of the practical processes and problems, to make your ideas a reality.

A1 Structure and format of a business plan

Although it seems daunting to organise your business plan into a formal structure, it is advisable to look at the plan in sections and to draft in stages. The final submission is not the most important aspect of planning – it is the process where the learning takes place. You will need to take time to develop, research, analyse and bring together your thoughts.

Choosing the right title

First, think about what you want to call your enterprise idea. The title can be important for improving your customers' awareness and initial opinions of your idea. Try to write an innovative slogan or **STRAP LINE**. A strap line is a short phrase summarising a product or service. You should try to catch the reader's attention.

You should research similar products and compare the names. Think about what is attractive to you, and ask other people what is attractive to them. It is important to think about your **TARGET MARKET** – a product aimed at a child will need a different focus to one that is aimed at an adult.

Practise

Write down as many slogans and words as you can from advertising campaigns that you know, using advertisements on the television or in newspapers.

1 What makes these words stand out, making you want to buy the product?

2 Write down as many words as you can that might sell your product or service.

3 Try to include them in the title or strap line for your product or service.

Some strap lines are so well known that people immediately associate them with the product, even when hearing them out of context

Executive summary paragraph

Now that you have the readers' attention, you will need to explain your idea and your product or service in more detail. The **EXECUTIVE SUMMARY** – a short section at the start of a report that sums up the main points – is often where a potential investor will decide whether to 'read on' or to 'ditch' your proposal. You have to convince the reader that your product or service is worth their investment. A typical executive summary includes:

- an explanation of how you came up with the product or service title
- your vision for your product or service, now and in the future
- your target market
- the **CONCEPT** (a concept is an idea to help sell or promote a product or service)
- your business structure, employees and type of ownership
- financing, investment and funding.

Finish the summary with an idea of where you see the business in five years. Describe how your product or service might evolve and what that will mean for your business.

The business vision or concept

You may want to produce a **VISION (OR MISSION) STATEMENT**. These are statements that describe the aims, goals and aspirations of a business.

You should think about how you might embed the main aims of your organisation into the mission statement. You need to think carefully about the wording and how you focus on the challenge of meeting customer needs, support the community and others (social aims), and the importance of making a profit.

Selling points

This is where you think about your **UNIQUE SELLING POINT (USP)**. This vision statement might appear on marketing materials, business documents or a company **WEBSITE**. It illustrates the aims of the business and promotes a feeling of trust and ethical working practices.

Vision statements vary according to the organisational structure and culture. In the case of a small enterprise, they can be simply a line of writing supported by a logo. Major business organisations may display strap lines, vision statements and mission statements on large advertising spaces such as buildings, bill boards and television.

The product or service

This is your opportunity to show exactly what your product or service is and what it does. Use photographs, diagrams and images. Your audience will not know your product or service, so it is important to be as clear and detailed as you can. If your product or service has a technological, scientific or technical element, it is important to use language effectively. The reader may not be familiar with specific words and references, and you need to communicate well to aid understanding.

Impact of the enterprise environment

Here, you will need to explain the 'place' of your product or service in the enterprise environment. Think about where it fits and its impact

Link it up

You can find more about the contents of this part of your business plan under 'Details of the product or service' in A2 of this unit.

on **STAKEHOLDERS**. Many environmental factors, internal and external, can impact on the success of a business. Think about all the points from Table 4.1 and how they might impact on your business either directly or indirectly.

Table 4.1: Environmental factors

Internal factors	External factors
Location	The economy
Vision, mission and aims	Political decisions
Beliefs, values, culture and ethics	Law and regulation
Management	Suppliers
Business structure	Competitors
Staffing, internal relationships	Technological advancement
Technology	Social

Summary of market research

Here, you will need to set out the findings of your **MARKET RESEARCH** on your product or service and the target market – the type of customers you hope to attract. This is an opportunity to show how much your product is needed and who will buy it. You can present your market research data in a variety of ways. Think about the diversity of your **CUSTOMER BASE** (the type of customers you have). Use charts, graphs and diagrams to present the information in a way that supports positivity and shows the reader why your customers want your product or service.

Remember that this is only a summary – you do not need to include all of the research that you carried out. However, you do need to have brought together the information on customer base, competitors and **MARKET SHARE** (the proportion of potential customers you hope to gain). This needs to be presented in a format that gives a clear picture of who was asked, why they were asked and what they said.

The marketing plan

Here, you will need to set out the route you will take to enter your target market and the promotion techniques you will use.

Routes to market

When establishing the route to your target market, think about the results of your market research.

a   How do your customers want you to sell to them?
b   How do you make it easy for them to buy from you?

You might make your decision on the basis of the **DEMOGRAPHIC** of your target market. A demographic is a collection of people sharing the same values or characteristics. Think about your customers' buying habits and where they are likely to access your product or service.

Explore a range of ideas, and think about the risks involved in selling through the wrong medium and targeting the wrong customers.

Link it up

Use the marketing plan you created in Unit 3 (B2).

You can find more about the contents of this part of your business plan in A2 later in this unit.

Figure 4.1: Possible routes to market

It is important that you communicate a clear vision of the customer base and the process of getting from development to delivery.

What if...?

Anna is selling a child's toy. The target market is not only the child, but also the parent and the grandparent. Anna has to convince the parent that the toy is safe, of value (educationally, emotionally or financially) and that, in terms of the child, it is an attractive product aimed at the appropriate age group.

1 Anna might think that the parent will be relatively young and so will be more likely to buy online. But what about older, perhaps less technologically experienced grandparents?

2 What is the risk if customers cannot buy the toy easily?

3 Why is it important for Anna to think about the range of consumers and the importance of identifying new and less obvious markets for the toy?

Promotion

Your plan must set out clearly the types of promotion you will use to advertise and market your product or service. You will need to show images of the types of **PROMOTIONAL** materials that you will use, such as:

- advertising through newspapers, magazines, posters and leaflets
- direct promotion through phone, letters and emails
- word of mouth through networking, meetings, conferences and industry groups
- media advertising through Facebook, Twitter, eBay, networks, apps and websites.

When presenting this information, set out clearly the costs involved and how the promotion relates to the product or service. All promotional materials should follow a consistent format and communicate the business's aims and vision.

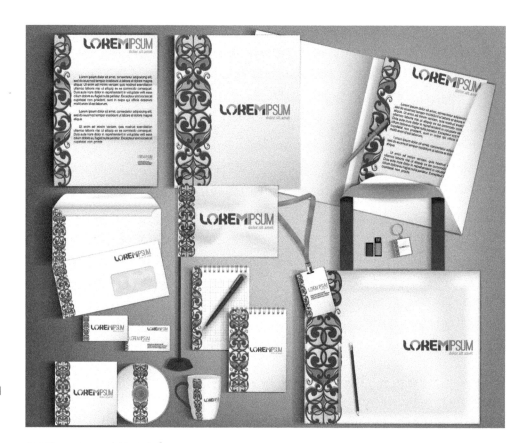

Before creating promotional materials, you will need to consider your brand

Link it up

You can find more about the contents of this part of your business plan under 'Promotional plan' in A2 later in this unit.

Figure 4.2: Having a good understanding of your finances is essential

Link it up

In Unit 3 (C1) you created your financial plan. Now is the time to think about how this information will be communicated to the readers of your business plan.

You can find more about the contents of this part of your business plan under 'Financial plan' in A2 later in this unit.

Summary of the financial plan

Here, you will need to provide a summary of your finance and funding.

Finance

Summarise how you will finance setting up and running your business. This might include your pricing strategy, costs, price and cost forecasts, budgets and cash-flow forecasts.

This section of your plan might be one of the most difficult for you to summarise. It is important when presenting financial information that the figures are accurate and that you fully understand the complex calculations. It is this part of the plan where you are likely to be asked questions by investors.

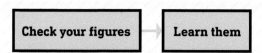

Funding

One of the main aims of your business plan is to present it to future investors. But it is important that you show in your plan that others are interested too and that you have thought carefully about how your business idea will be funded.

It would be useful, here, to present a range of ideas you have about funding and who might be a stakeholder in your business. How much funding you need for your business will be linked to your financial forecasting and will depend on the size of your business venture.

Goodwill

It is good to think of stakeholders as being of equal value – this shows an ethical approach to working practices. Remember that many businesses depend on the goodwill provided by family, friends and others. Employees have a huge stake in the business and are often **SHAREHOLDERS**, owning a share of the business and having a say in how the business is run. Businesses that use this model include John Lewis and the Co-operative Society.

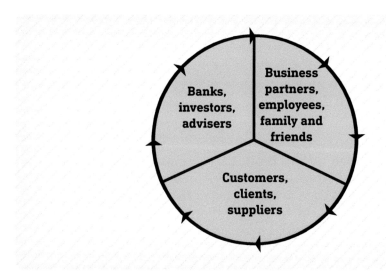

Figure 4.3: It is important that you consider all the stakeholders in your business, including family and friends

Risk analysis

Most business ventures run into problems at the start. It is one thing to have detailed plans in place, but another to carry them out effectively. Here, you will need to set out how you will deal with any problems that might come up.

You might be asked about unforeseen problems and contingency plans, so it is best to have evaluated this information beforehand, and include it in your business plan to show that you have thought through some strategies. Research online to look at a range of risk analysis forms that are used by businesses. Companies often have to design their own forms to meet specific requirements, because all products and services are different.

Link it up

You can find more about the contents of this part of your business plan under 'Risk analysis' in A2 later in this unit.

Business targets

Here, you will need to show that you understand the importance of planning, target setting and review. The reader is likely to be experienced in planning, either through their role in an organisation or as an entrepreneur.

It is important to have an idea about where you want to be with your business and what you want to do. One way of doing this is to set clear long- and short-term targets with timings. In your business plan you can show this as a timeline or as an action plan.

Link it up

You can find more about the contents of this part of your business plan under 'SMART targets' in A2 later in this unit.

Appendices

At this point, you will have undertaken a great deal of research and gathered a large range of materials. You can add supporting information to your business plan in the appendices (a section at the end of a book or document for 'appended' or additional material), but it is important you include only the most relevant and appropriate information. The appendices should always support the plan and might include:

- market research, e.g. a **SAMPLE** of **QUESTIONNAIRES**
- examples of marketing materials
- location maps showing competitors
- analytical data not presented in the plan, e.g. statistics from surveys
- financial forecasts and financial planning documents.

A2 Contents and presentation of a business plan

Your business plan should have a structure that is logical to the reader (audience), be formatted appropriately and be presented accurately. Research business plans online for ideas on the various formats you can use. Consider the type of plan that best suits your vision, product or service.

One of the most effective ways of producing accurate materials that are 'FIT FOR PURPOSE' is to follow a process of drafting and editing. 'Fit for purpose' means that it must be relevant to the customer base and designed to meet the needs of the target market. Make sure that you set drafting targets (for example in the form of an action plan). Set timings for each step of the process with clear dates so that you meet deadlines.

Figure 4.4 sets out how you could use the drafting and editing process for presenting your business plan to your assessor. It is important to remember, however, that you are *not* allowed seek feedback from your tutor until *after* you have presented your plan.

First draft	**Initial feedback**	**Second draft**
Decide on title, headings. Choose an appropriate font. Write a brief paragraph under each heading. Read through for accuracy.	Work in pairs to share ideas and get feedback on your first draft.	Add detail to the content, expand on the writing. Include relevant diagrams and images.

Final draft	**Editing**	**Group feedback**
Prepare your business plan for final feedback and amendments. This should be almost finished. Read through carefully for spelling, punctuation and grammar.	Add to your business plan taking into account all feedback and ideas from colleagues.	In groups, swap business plans, give feedback and share ideas. Use a peer assessment checklist so that comments are documented.

Final feedback	**Final copy**
Share your plan with mentors and advisers. Consider recording the conversation to ensure that you have all the detail you need to complete your plan.	Produce a final copy of your plan, which should include all headings, content, images, diagrams and supporting information. Your plan should be presented to your assessor so that it is as professional-looking as possible.

Figure 4.4: Drafting and editing your business plan

Contents

In the final draft of your business plan, make sure you have all the elements in place and clear and detailed contents.

Details of the product or service

When presenting the details of your new idea in your business plan, you will need to describe your product or service, explain it, show its possible application and set out how you have evaluated its effectiveness.

Explain how your product or service will benefit customers. If other similar products and services are already on the market, use this part of your business plan to explain how your product or service is different or complements the existing TRENDS.

Visual impact

Focus on the impact it will have when introduced to the customer base. Describe the product or service visually and give the specifications, colour and size. Visual appearance can be one of your main selling points.

If you are focusing on a service, you will need to describe and explain the service in detail. Think about what the service actually looks like to a customer. This can be difficult because it is hard to illustrate service as a tangible thing. It will help to look at the people who will deliver the service: their appearance, communication and selling technique.

Show its potential application by explaining how it works, the technical details and how the product is made or the service is developed. You need to explain process or production plans and your strategy for developing the product or service up to the point at which it is sold.

If you are promoting a 'service' it is important to think about what this might look like to a customer

Market research

Be honest about competitors, and show an analysis of other markets, particularly in terms of location. Maps help to illustrate where similar businesses are situated in relation to yours. Physical distance can make a difference when you are making a case for investment. Show how you are different. Make sure you always show how your USP has been informed by your market research – and how your USP meets the needs of your customers, identified through your market research.

It is important that the audience knows that you have a viable product or service, that it will sell and that people will buy it. It is also important that you have a clear understanding of your customer base, your competitors and what market share you can hope to control.

Think about the age and gender of your target customers

Link it up

You will have created a marketing plan in Unit 3. Did your market research bring out ideas from your potential customer base?

Customer base

Who are your customers? What is their:

- age?
- gender?
- culture?
- background?

Competitors

Who are your competitors? What is their:

- location?
- share of the market?
- viability?
- customer base?
- marketing strategy?

Potential market share

Is there room for your product or service in your target market? Set out the results of your research into:

- comparisons of similar products or services
- whether it attracts a different demographic
- trends
- calculations based on evidence-based research.

Promotional plan

How you promote your product will depend on the results of your market research and your analysis of promotional techniques. This information should be summarised in your plan. Ensure that you cover all of the four Ps in your plan – product, price, place and promotion. You might want to highlight each of these separately.

The four Ps will help inform other parts of your plan. For example, price will influence your financial plan, and place will influence your routes to market. Although these are distinct sections of the plan, make sure that the points you mention here are also reflected elsewhere, and vice versa.

The promotion you use needs to be fit for purpose. It is important to think about where you will advertise and that you use the most appropriate method of advertising (promotion). For example, if the purpose is to sell country clothing, advertising in urban areas will have risks, although the location of golf clubs, equestrian centres, outdoor activity centres or city farms might influence your decision.

Why do you think you need to know as much as possible about your customer base?

It is important to include an outline of your **PROMOTIONAL PLAN** within your business plan. The plan should explain your campaign for your product or service and include a justification of your choices in terms of marketing, advertising and the use of digital media.

Financial plan

Use graphs, charts and diagrams to illustrate the following.

- *Costs* – include all the relevant costs for your product or service, and double check these before any pitch. Costs, such as rental costs for premises, can change at any time, and you should always present the latest.
- **REVENUE STREAMS** – make sure that the ways your business will make money are all still feasible. Your later research might have led to revisions to your original idea, or an early idea might need removing.
- **SALES PROJECTIONS** (an estimate of how much you expect to sell over a particular time period) – as with costs, you should always check that these are the most up to date when presenting them. A shift in your market, such as a competitor opening nearby since your original projections, can affect your figures.
- *Projected* **INCOME STATEMENT** *and cash-flow forecast* – double check your figures on these. You will likely want to provide these as separate, headed, full-page documents.
- **START-UP COSTS** *and finance costs* – make sure you're clear on what costs need to be allocated where, and again check that nothing has changed.

Risk analysis

You need to identify potential risks to your new venture and evaluate these in your business plan. This is important because it will help you to analyse potential problems and solutions. Look at all aspects of the plan:

- aims and vision
- marketing and promotion
- finance
- target setting
- production
- sales
- investment.

Think about how you are going to present this information. One way might be to develop a table with possible problems and solutions linked to various parts of your plan.

Table 4.2: Solutions to risks that might arise in business

Possible risk	Possible solution
A cheaper product or service comes onto the market	• Sell on quality over price • Compromise quality of your product or service to produce it more cheaply • Make your product or service different • Develop the product or service further
A similar business opens in the same location	• Work with your competitors to share the market • Change your marketing strategy, focus and vision • Develop new business • Move your business • Research to ensure there is room for both businesses
Loss of trained staff	• Evaluate working practices, relationships, salaries • Employ more staff and re-train • Offer leaving staff a better working package
Costs go up dramatically	• Move the business • Make staff redundant • Diversify • Review present costings to make savings

Link it up

Look back to 'Promotion' in A1 of this unit for examples of promotional materials you might include in your plan.

In Unit 2 (C1) you learned about the marketing mix of product, place, price and promotion (the four Ps).

In Unit 3 you produced a promotional plan and a financial plan. You will need to summarise the research and information effectively to present it within your business plan.

Link it up

You will have the figures from Unit 3 (C1), but since writing your financial plan you might have adapted your ideas, so check that everything is still appropriate. Add as much detail to your plan as possible.

Practise

Try to focus on solutions and not on the problems and consider:

1 What will you do if a similar product or service cheaper than yours comes onto the market?

2 What will you do if a similar business to yours opens in the same location?

3 What will you do if your trained staff leave?

4 What will you do if your costs go up dramatically?

SMART targets

Make sure that your long- and short-term business targets match your aims and vision for the business. When presenting this information, it is useful to think about **SMART TARGETS** and use Specific, Measurable, Achievable, Realistic and Time-bound as headings. This will help you to focus on quality aims to help your business in terms of growth and performance.

You will need to think about the focus of your targets, for example financial performance indicators could include:

- targets around **TURNOVER** (the amount of **REVENUE** and sales turned over by a business) – expectations, **INCOME** and expenditure, time-bound
- targets around profit – forecasts, goals, future projections
- targets around sales – **PROFIT MARGINS** (profit as a percentage of turnover), forecasts, data, figures
- targets around output – expansion, balances, investment.

Non-financial indicators

You should also consider non-financial performance indicators. Examples of non-financial targets might include commitments to equality in the workforce, working with a charity or supporting environmental initiatives.

All of the above can be measured by reviewing the achievement against specific aims that are linked to the mission statement or business objectives.

You may find it useful to set out your targets in a SMART format, for example:

Link it up

In Unit 1 (C3) you learned about SMART objectives.

In Unit 3 (B3) you planned a costed promotional campaign based on SMART promotional objectives.

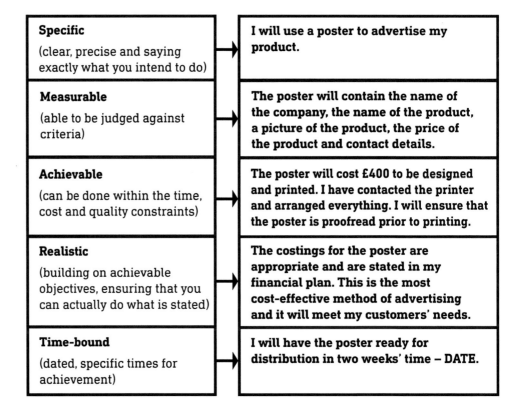

Specific (clear, precise and saying exactly what you intend to do)	I will use a poster to advertise my product.
Measurable (able to be judged against criteria)	The poster will contain the name of the company, the name of the product, a picture of the product, the price of the product and contact details.
Achievable (can be done within the time, cost and quality constraints)	The poster will cost £400 to be designed and printed. I have contacted the printer and arranged everything. I will ensure that the poster is proofread prior to printing.
Realistic (building on achievable objectives, ensuring that you can actually do what is stated)	The costings for the poster are appropriate and are stated in my financial plan. This is the most cost-effective method of advertising and it will meet my customers' needs.
Time-bound (dated, specific times for achievement)	I will have the poster ready for distribution in two weeks' time – DATE.

Figure 4.5: Using SMART targets will help you focus on your aims

Link your targets to specific parts of your plan to make sure that all elements are moving forward in terms of future expectations. Make sure that when targets are set they are followed through and monitored – it is easy to set targets, but showing how they are evaluated and analysed is more difficult.

Presentation of the business plan

The final presentation of your business plan is important to the success of your business. Make sure you understand all aspects of the content. It should be a detailed document that is fit for purpose in terms of the audience. It should also be useful as a tool to take you forward to the next stage of developing your business enterprise.

Look at your plan through the eyes of the investor who will read it. Remember the importance of first impressions. Think about the cover, the sections, the headings, the use of appropriate fonts and the overall presentation.

Numbered sections

Make sure that everything is in an appropriate order and there is a natural flow to the document. Numbering sections is useful for referencing and to help focus on individual parts of the document. Your business plan will be an extensive document, and reference points such as numbered sections will help the reader to revisit content. Imagine you were talking on the phone to someone who was asking questions about your plan and think about how you would answer questions on particular aspects of it – this is a way of directing people to relevant points.

Consistent use of fonts, headings and page numbering

It is important to number pages – imagine your reader dropping the document and not being able to put them back in the right order. Think about the placement of the page numbers – this might be influenced by how the document will be bound. Make it as easy for the reader as you can.

Using the same font throughout your document will help to make it look professional. However, you can use different fonts to highlight important points for the reader to note.

Size of headings

Keep headings in different sections the same size, but have sub-headings decrease in size to help the reader identify where sub-sections start and end.

Use capital letters, underlining, italics and bullet points to break down information and make it more interesting to the reader.

Layout and use of graphics, charts and diagrams

Use a range of graphics, charts and diagrams to illustrate the points you are trying to make. Choose your images carefully to make sure they are the most appropriate methods of display.

> # Marketing Plan
>
> ## Market research
>
> - Customer base
> - Competitors
> - Potential market share

Figure 4.6: An example of how fonts and size can be used to illustrate the importance of key points

---

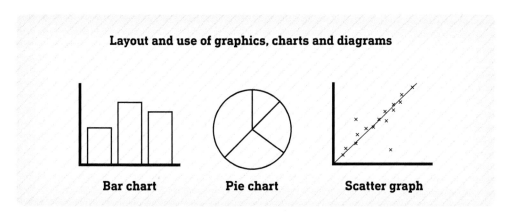

Layout and use of graphics, charts and diagrams

| Bar chart | Pie chart | Scatter graph |

Figure 4.7: Graphics can have a strong visual impact

Link it up

Look back to 'Appendices' in A1 of this unit for examples of content you might include here.

Research online and look at a range of documents to get ideas about layout. The most important point is that the document is presented in a way that meets the needs of the audience and to best describe your business idea in a way that makes a positive impression.

The purpose and content of appendices

The purpose of including documents in the appendices is to give the reader the opportunity to look in more detail at some of the practical aspects of the research you have done. It is also an opportunity to include some of the documents or data that are not appropriate in the main document but that still provide useful information.

Skills and knowledge check

- [ ] What is a strap line?
- [ ] What should the market research section of your plan include?
- [ ] List three types of graphics you might find on a business plan.
- [ ] List the main sections that your business plan should include.

- ◯ I can write a vision statement for my business.
- ◯ I can present a risk analysis highlighting problems and solutions.
- ◯ I can use images appropriately to support communication.
- ◯ I can present financial information in a variety of ways, including graphs, charts and diagrams.

Ready for assessment

You will have produced a detailed business plan that has been carefully checked and is now ready for assessment. The business plan will form the basis of your pitch for the next learning aim.

Are you ready?

Check that your document is fit for purpose. The purpose is to produce a document that will help you to present a pitch to investors. The plan should be structured, integrated and detailed. It should also include an analysis of risks.

Checklist for final presentation of your document:

> **CHECKLIST**
>
> - [ ] Have you checked the content to make sure everything is in place and that all the components are clear and cannot be misunderstood?
> - [ ] Have you checked the spelling, punctuation and grammar?
> - [ ] Have you discussed your plan with mentors, work-based colleagues and peers?
> - [ ] Have you let others read your plan and provide feedback?
> - [ ] Have you amended your plan based on the feedback given?
> - [ ] Are you pleased with the end result – does it look professional?
>
> **Reflection**
>
> Think about the process that you have just gone through and write about what you learned. Are you proud of your business plan and how it will help you in the future?

B Present a business pitch to an audience including a potential investor or business adviser

Your business plan is written, and you have all the information you need to be able to plan your pitch to investors and advisers.

B1 Features of a business pitch

The pitch is the formal presentation of your business plan to an audience. The audience will probably be a range of people such as colleagues, investors, advisers, employers, mentors, assessors and peers.

Preparation

Read through your business plan again. Think about how you are going to present this information.
- Research different presentation methods.
- Research alternatives to PowerPoint® – PowToon, Prezi, Keynote, Prezentit.

Preparation

When you have decided on your presentation tool, make sure that you know how to use it effectively. Practise: it is worth spending some time understanding the technology.

Preparation

Once you have mastered the technology you need to draft out the information from your business plan into your chosen medium. It is important here that you select the most relevant information and images. One pitfall is to copy in too much information.

Practice

Once you are happy that everything is in place, you will need to practise the presentation and edit the content. Make sure you know the content, particularly the finance information. Aim to do the presentation in 30 minutes including the time for questions. This is difficult, time it carefully and cut it accordingly. You may find it useful to video the presentation.

Feedback

It is important to get feedback on the first run through. If you are using technology, your audience will see where you are using too much information or identify the gaps. The audience should have a copy of your business plan. Encourage questioning at this stage. This will help to prepare you for the 'real pitch'.

Practice

This is the final run through, taking into account your feedback from the first practice. You should have amended the presentation. You need, at this point, to think about what you are going to wear, where you are going to stand, if you need extra tools such as your notes, handouts, copies of business plans, flip charts, pens, notebooks, tables for people to sit at. Arrange the room to suit the presentation style and ensure that you are comfortable. Check the technology and ensure that support is there should you need it. This practice may be used for formative assessment and the feedback you receive is your final chance to perfect your presentation.

Preparation

Have a checklist to make sure that everything is in place – that the technology works; that the room is prepared; that your notes, handouts and other supporting materials are prepared and photocopied; that you have decided what to wear; that you know the content of the presentation without reading from slides; that you are prepared for questions.

Figure 4.8: Allowing plenty of time to prepare and practise your pitch could make a big difference to how well it is received

Pitching

The pitch is your opportunity to showcase your product or service. It is a chance for you to get the funding you need to start your business. This might be your only opportunity to tell people what you can do, so the pitch is crucial to the success of your business.

When thinking about planning and preparing for a presentation, it is useful to work through a process. This will help you to order things appropriately and to identify gaps.

Know your audience

Your audience will want to know that your product or service is a good investment. You need to be confident that you understand all aspects of your business plan and that you have a viable and profitable idea that is worth their attention. They will want to know that you have the expertise within your team of employees (or potential employees) to be able to produce and sell the product or service.

It is important to vary the tone of your pitch according to the range of people in your audience. You might present your pitch several times to different audiences, so it is important to adapt and modify your body language, tone and focus.

Table 4.3: Presenting to different audiences

Audience	Approach, tone, context, focus
Investors, bank managers, advisers, mentors	• A professional approach • Direct tone, presenting facts, detail, figures • A formal context • Focus on selling product/service to influence investment
Family, friends, donators, business partners	• A more relaxed approach but still professional • Presenting facts and detail • Semi-formal context – highlighting ethical working practices • Focus on selling ideas to get support and encouragement; a need for validation
Peers, assessors, tutors	• A professional approach • Semi-relaxed tone but presenting facts and figures • Assessment context, so ensure all content of specification is covered • Focus on covering assessment criteria

Link it up

In Unit 3 (C1) you covered this in detail, and the information will be clearly identified in your financial plan. The important thing is that you understand the figures and are prepared for the difficult questions.

Know your figures

Prospective investors will need assurances that their money will be safe and invested securely. If they are to be stakeholders in your business, they will want to analyse your figures. Be prepared – you might get asked difficult questions about costings, cash flow, projections and profit margins.

If you are presenting graphs, charts, diagrams or statistics, make sure that that all of the images are supported by clear data, to show that you have researched appropriately and that your information is accurate, realistic and up to date.

Practising the presentation

You will need to practise your presentation several times before you are confident enough to deliver it without constantly referring to notes, reading from a script or referring to slides. Think about your audience – you could be presenting to family, friends, colleagues or peers. You may want to develop feedback sheets to encourage the audience to make suggestions for improvement.

It is worth spending time going over the content and editing the slides, handouts and notes. If you decide to write a script, which can be a useful tool, it is important not to take it to the presentation with you, but to memorise it, pick out the important points and put them either on a list that you can glance at during the presentation or on a set of cards.

Critical evaluation

Use your phone camera or other technology to record or video yourself. Critically analyse your performance, checking for:

- body language and mannerisms
- tone of voice and sound projection
- use of technology
- appearance
- use of language.

Be honest with yourself – use the information in the next section to review your performance, and revise your pitch to improve it.

Presentation

Oral

Oral presentations can be difficult, and the need for practice and feedback sessions cannot be underestimated. It is not always easy to stand up in front of people and talk.

Practise

Focus on one section of your business plan, for example your financial plan.

1 Time yourself and talk for one minute about financing your product/ service – record yourself.

2 Listen to the recording and make notes to improve – revise as appropriate.

3 Time yourself and talk for two minutes on the same topic – record yourself.

4 Listen to the recording and make further notes – revise as appropriate.

5 Repeat for three minutes.

6 Listen to your three-minute recording and analyse your skills (tone, pace, use of language, understanding of topic).

Think about your voice in terms of projection and tone. You will need to think about the language you use to communicate – use only the business terminology that you understand. Recording your voice will help you to evaluate yourself and improve.

Visual

How you are seen visually is an important aspect of any pitch. You will need to dress appropriately. This does not necessarily mean you have to wear a business suit, but you must think about your audience's expectations. Your type of product or service may determine the way you are dressed. For example, it might be appropriate to wear sportswear if you are demonstrating a new piece of sports equipment, or chef's whites if you are selling a new recipe and demonstrating cookery. If you are promoting any kind of garment, you would be expected to wear something from the range.

Mannerisms

Some personal traits and mannerisms are difficult to change, and people are often unaware of some of their own behaviours. When presenting, these can become exaggerated and draw attention away from what you are saying.

These include:

- body language traits (folding arms, gesturing, fidgeting)
- eye contact (reading from slides, not talking directly to the audience)
- position (standing in front of slides, moving too much or too little).

So it is important to practise your presentation as many times as you can. Using your phone or a video to tape your presentation is one way of making yourself aware of your personal traits and behaviours. Then practise changing negative or distracting behaviours to improve your presentation skills.

Computer projection and slide shows

When deciding on your presentation tools, explore a range of methods and think about the advantages and disadvantages of using each one. PowerPoint® is the most popular method of presenting information to audiences, but it is not the only tool. It might make a good impression to use something newer and more innovative, but it is more important to choose something that displays your information to the best advantage. Research online to find out the latest techniques and software.

Table 4.4: Presentation software

Method	Advantages	Disadvantages
PowerPoint®	- Quick and easy to use. - Images are easily inserted. - Popular and understood by all. - Easily available with Microsoft Office®. - Can use speaker notes to help with design and support communication.	- Does not show innovation in thinking about tools to use. - Can be boring if too many words are used. - Is criticised by many as being overused.
Prezi	- Gives movement to presentations. - Can offer innovative ways of displaying and presenting information. - Good for presenting a range of images.	- Tendency to overdo the images and can bombard the audience with moving diagrams, photos and charts. - Must be used effectively.
PowToon	- Innovative in design. - Free to download. - Easy to use. - Popular alternative to PowerPoint® slides. - Animation focus. - Can look very professional, but needs careful design. - Good for storytelling.	- Must suit the presentation topic. - Can come across as childlike if not used carefully. - Not always useful to communicate facts. - May need to upgrade to be able to access easily.
SlideRocket	- Available through Microsoft. - Upgrade of PowerPoint®. - Quality product. - Innovative in design and offers the opportunity to deliver high-quality presentations.	- Expensive. - More complex than other methods and may need to spend time learning how to use it.

The use of other presentation tools

A range of computer-generated presentations allow you to add speaker notes automatically. These notes will help you to plan what you are going to communicate to the audience and will also act as a reminder to you.

Rather than try to put all the written communication onto slides, it is better to use handouts to give further information. Try to use no more than six bullet points per slide, to avoid overloading both you and the audience and to aid focus. You can use handheld cards to help you expand on the bullet points as you move through the presentation. Audiences like handouts that they can refer to and take away to read later. You can use the handouts to show images that might be difficult to interpret on a screen.

Flip charts

Using flip charts is a useful way of engaging the audience and writing up points they are making. If, for example, you are asked a question you cannot answer, you can write it onto the flip chart and return to it later, making sure that all questions are answered. This will show that you are willing to research the answer and get back to the questioner.

How to respond to potential investors' questions

There are several ways that you can plan questioning into your presentation.

Table 4.5: Responding to questions

Method	Advantages	Disadvantages
Questioning throughout the presentation, pausing at the end of sections.	You can answer instantly and move on. It helps to break down the presentation and can be a more relaxed approach.	It can be disruptive and take you away from your train of thought. You can get a difficult person in the audience who constantly asks questions, and this can be hard to manage. It may distract to the point of not completing your pitch.
Asking for questions to be written down throughout the presentation and giving the answers at the end.	This can give you time to consider your answers, particularly if there is time for a break in the presentation. Sometimes when questions are written down they are easier to understand and you can ask for clarification.	You may have lost your train of thought and not remember the context of the question. The questions are anonymous and can be more difficult to answer and more complex.
Allowing time at the end for all questions.	The questions can be very focused and you can manage the time more easily. If there are a lot of questions you can target specific people in the audience, ensuring that there are a range of contributors.	You may be asked questions that relate to the very start of the presentation, and it is difficult sometimes to remember all the information (if you know your slides well, you can return to the specific information).

It is important that you make clear at the beginning of the presentation what the method of questioning will be. For example, you could say: 'There will be 10 minutes at the end of the presentation for questions – would you please be kind and save all questions until I have completed my pitch?'

Things do not always go to plan, and if someone has a question during your pitch, it is important to answer straight away or to 'park' the question (add it to a flip chart or make a note of it) and answer it at the end of your pitch. This will help you to keep your flow and not get too distracted.

Listening skills

Hearing the question accurately and understanding what is being asked is vital if you are to answer successfully with confidence. An audience should have respect for the deliverer and always ask questions that are relevant and in language that is clearly understood – but occasionally someone will use technical language.

It is never a problem to ask for clarification, and this is better than trying to answer something which you do not really understand.

What to listen for

Remember to:
- *listen for* specific terminology
- *listen for* the meaning of the question

- *listen for* the expectations of the answer
- *listen for* clarity
- *listen for* understanding.

But, never listen for the argument. If a question is confrontational in content, stay calm and bring the context back to your presentation, giving facts, figures and specifics.

When responding to questions, try to have all your facts and figures to hand

Formulating appropriate responses and asking for clarification

When responding to questions, be confident and calm, and answer as clearly as possible. Try not to give out too much information. Allow for others to add to the question to clarify, or perhaps ask for more detail.

Difficult questions

When answering a question, listen first, then refer to the words used in the question – this will help you to focus your mind on what is being asked. Be ready for the difficult questions – have all of your facts and figures at your fingertips. It is useful to have handouts with:

- risk analysis and contingencies listed
- facts and figures
- cash flow.

You will probably be asked questions about your financial planning, so it is vital that you have a clear understanding of forecasts and profit margins.

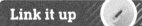

Link it up

In Unit 3 (C1) you will have prepared your financial plan, and this information will be in your business plan. It will be useful to go over these figures carefully before your pitch.

Table 4.6: Examples of questions and responses

Example of a question	Example of an appropriate response
'I noticed in your market research that you only used 20 questionnaires. What were the reasons for using such a small sample?'	'We covered all of the target market within the questions we asked and gained clear and relevant data. Had it not given us the information, we would have widened the sample.'
'What will you do if your product proves to be too expensive for the target market and a cheaper product is available elsewhere?'	'Our contingency plans include product development and researching cheaper raw materials. You will see on your handout that we have done a full risk analysis and identified probable risks in development costs.'
'What is the value of your product above anything else that is on the market?'	'Our product is innovative and meets the needs of a specific target market. There is only one other similarly designed product on the market, and ours is 20% cheaper to produce and of better quality.'
'What is your USP?'	'Our USP is: "We will promise quality and value with a customer money-back guarantee." This is unique because none of our competitors make this promise.'

Practise

In pairs, practise asking questions about your draft business plans and then feed back on how well you felt your questions were answered. Make sure that you ask a range of questions, including some potentially difficult ones – you can use Table 4.6 as a starting point.

B2 Presentation skills used in a business pitch

Communication in all its forms is crucial to the success of running any business.

What if...?

Brenda and Bill work in research and development. They have been discussing a new idea and want to present it to management. They want to develop a new range of sweets and biscuits. This is going to be expensive, but they feel that it may be attractive to a new and wider demographic and therefore improve sales. They are nervous about their presentation and want to make a good impression.

1　How do you think they should go about presenting their new idea?

2　How can they make a positive impact?

3　What skills and techniques will they have to develop?

4　What technology might they use?

5　What could go wrong, and what contingency plans should they put in place?

Presentation, behaviour and conduct

You are going to pitch your new product or service idea to an audience. That audience will make decisions about you based on how well you are prepared, your attitude, your clothing and your professionalism.

Positive attitude

Try to:

- smile at your audience, look happy to be there, welcome them
- show you are confident – talk with authority and understanding
- stand up straight with good eye contact
- show a good work ethic through your responses and your willingness to work hard to make your idea successful
- show you care about what you are presenting and that you truly believe in your product/service.

Preparation

In the days before your presentation, try to make sure you:

- know your presentation – read and learn everything
- know your facts and figures, and understand the calculations
- prepare your notes and keep them short (you know your presentation)
- practise your presentation in front of a range of audiences and get feedback
- think about how you are going to set the room up, in terms of where you are going to stand, how you will arrange the tables and chairs and what handouts and materials you will want to lay out for the audience.

Attire

Dress to meet the expectations of the audience – learn beforehand as much as you can about them – a traditional audience of business owners will look for cleanliness, smart attire and clean shoes. A younger audience may expect a different approach, but do not underestimate the power of appearance. Dress to impress.

Smart business-like clothing will give you a professional appearance if you are giving a presentation in a formal setting

Professional approach

The audience will expect a professional attitude throughout. When presenting to an audience, professionals will always have a mature, adult approach.

Table 4.7: Dos and don'ts for presentations

Dos	Don'ts
Dress appropriately	Use negative body language, shrugging, folded arms, fidgeting
Be honest	Imply devious business methods through misinformation or poor eye contact
Respect your audience and their experience	Be off-hand or argue points when feedback is given
Be positive	Be negative about your business idea or your colleagues
Show positive traits, reliability, integrity and competence	Give the impression that you don't know what you are doing, through lack of confidence
Listen carefully	Ignore advice, feedback, or pretend you understand a question if you don't
Be work focused	Give the impression of laziness by over-delegation
Be well prepared	Underestimate the need to practise and the importance of having everything in place for your presentation

Communication skills

In delivering your business pitch, you will use a range of communication skills. You will not identify these skills individually, because they will be embedded in what you are saying. You will naturally communicate through your body language and your interaction with the audience.

Think about the communication tools that you will use – your non-verbal skills, your voice and the choice of words and actions you will use to communicate your business vision. The opening line to your pitch is when you introduce yourself, tell the audience who you are and what you represent. When you have this introduction in place it will calm your nerves and give you a 'starting point'.

Using language suitable for the audience

The type of language you use – on slides, handouts and leaflets and the spoken word – will impact positively or negatively on how well the audience understands you and whether they see you as a good communicator.

Do not try to impress with the over-use of business terminology and jargon. Aim your use of language at the level of the least experienced person in the group.

Your audience will pick up on your body language, so try to look positive and confident even if you are feeling nervous

Body language and gestures

During your presentation you will be the centre of attention. You are the 'front of house' speaker for your business – you are there to promote your product or service to the people who will decide whether it is a viable investment or whether it needs further development.

You will have practised your presentation many times and received feedback from peers, tutors, mentors and others. This will have given you the opportunity to examine positive and negative personal traits, such as:

- posture
- head and hand movements

- fidgeting and movement
- facial expressions
- eye contact with the audience.

Voice

Use your voice to convey the content of what you want to say clearly and concisely to your audience. Your voice is important because it can show how confident you are in your enterprise idea.

Variation in tone

When speaking, emphasise certain words and aspects of your presentation. Use differences in tone to give 'life' to your words and keep the audience interested.

Practise

Think about the opening line or introduction to your pitch. You could start by saying:

'Welcome everyone, my name is .... and I am here today to tell you about a new and exciting opportunity.'

Try saying the sentence in different ways with the emphasis on different words. Use the tone, volume and expression to make what you are saying more interesting. Practise in front of a mirror.

Work on coming across as confident, assured and professional.

Appropriate pace, volume and projection

Do not be frightened of silence. Pausing is a skill used to emphasise points and give the audience a chance to think about what you are saying. Speak slowly, clearly and at a volume appropriate to the size of the room and the number of people present. Project your voice simply by speaking clearly and looking to the back of the room.

Use pace to keep the flow going throughout your pitch. For example, you could use a clock in the room to work out roughly where you want to be in the presentation at what time.

Eye contact

Eye contact with the audience is important. Try to make everyone in the room think that you are talking to each of them as an individual. Avoid:

- looking at and reading the presentation (always work from notes if you need to)
- turning your back on the audience
- staring at specific individuals
- looking up at the ceiling or down at the floor
- giving the impression of not listening to the questions or comments.

Position

Think about your distance from the audience and where you will stand. Think about where you will put any equipment you are using, such as tables and flipcharts. If you can, plan the room layout beforehand, making sure that chairs and tables are organised to meet the needs of the audience – it might be appropriate to sit around a table, or you might want your audience in a semicircle in front of you.

It can be intimidating to have your audience sat behind tables as if they are judging you! Although the needs of the audience are crucial, you will still have some control, so also think about yourself to make sure that the room supports your own needs as a presenter.

Using business terminology

If you have to use technical language because of the nature and design of a specific product or service, you should always explain meanings to help the audience understand.

Table 4.8: Jargon buster

Business jargon	Alternative
'My organisation believes in functional relative matrix approaches'	'My company believes that departments should work together'
'The solution can only be functional policy mobility'	'The solution is to look at a practical policy that is flexible'
'It's time to revamp and reboot our "Outside the box" management contingencies'	'It's time to look at new and innovative ways of doing things'

Remember that you do not have to use big words to impress people. Never use words that you do not understand – you might be asked to explain what you mean.

Signalling the end of the pitch

At the end of your pitch, you will probably feel confident enough to answer further questions and take part in discussion. To signal this point, there are a few options you can consider.

a   Put a slide at the end of the presentation saying 'Thank you for your time' and refer to it.
b   Say simply: 'I am coming to the end of the pitch and want to give you an opportunity to ask more detailed questions. Thank you for your support.'
c   If time has overrun, and especially if you have taken a lot of questions during the pitch, you can say: 'I can't take any more questions now as we have run out of time, but if you write them down I will be happy to contact you with the answers at a later date.'

Handling questions

Always be polite when answering questions. If a question seems to you to be inappropriate, it might not seem that way to the person asking it. Deal with each question individually, and answer to the best of your ability. If you do not know how to respond accurately, simply say that you will find out the answer and get back to the questioner later – and always make a note there and then of the question, to show that you intend to deal with it at a later date.

It might sometimes be difficult to know what is actually being asked. If you do not understand a question, simply say something like 'I am sorry but I don't understand the question', and the questioner will often re-phrase. If there is just one part of the question you do not understand, for example a technical term, you could say something like: 'Can I just clarify what you mean by …?' Remember that no one in the audience wants to see you fail.

Your final words

Use your final words to politely thank the audience for their time and initiate the next step, which could be a phone call or a further meeting. Here are a few examples.

a   'I want to thank you for your time and hope that we can work together in the future.'
b   'Thank you for your interest in my plans. If you would like to make an appointment to see me to discuss things further, please call me.'
c   'Thank you. Please get in touch with me if you have any further questions or want to discuss my plans in more detail.'

The main aim of any presentation intended to impress an audience or sell a product or service is to leave the audience wanting more.

Use of notes

Notes will help you focus and boost your confidence. These might be postcards, notes on slides, a slide list or just helpful words noted down.

When you first start to give presentations and pitch an idea, nerves can take over and your mind might go blank. This is when having an aid, such as notes, becomes especially useful. Try:

- writing a few main points for expanding on your slides – one card per slide
- writing the slide numbers and a few bullet points next to each one
- having a print out of the slides in front of you with handwritten notes – it would be useful to give the audience a copy of these slides, too, so that they can make their own notes for questions
- having a print out of the slides with the notes pages, which you can format when you prepare the slides.

Use of visual aids

What visual aids will you have available for your presentation?

Link it up

Look back at 'Computer projection/ slide show' in B1 in this unit for advantages and disadvantages of a range of presentation software.

Choosing presentation software

Make sure that you are familiar with all aspects of the presentation software and that you fully understand the strengths and limitations of the tools available within it.

Clarity

Your message needs to be clear and free from misunderstanding. Check that your written words are clear, are readable and that they accurately convey what you are trying to say in as few words as possible.

Impact

Use fonts, images and diagrams to best advantage. Make sure that every slide you use impacts on the audience. You can impress the audience through the use of colours, shapes, innovative diagrams and images, and photos. YouTube and video clips will have a strong impact, as long as they are useful to the audience.

Use of graphics and appropriate images

Using graphics and images is a good way of breaking up the monotony of using words. Illustrate your finance information with diagrams, charts and graphs. This will allow the audience to examine your figures and see the reality of cash flow and projected profits.

Pictures and moving diagrams will allow your audience to see your vision 'brought to life'. These will also show that you can use technology effectively to illustrate your points, and that you are thinking about the needs of the audience in terms of how they process information.

Legibility of text

It is vital that you correct all spelling and grammar errors before your pitch. Also make sure that your presentation can be read easily from the audience seating area.

Do not get overambitious by using too many colours, changes of font or irrelevant images that do not support the text. If using diagrams, make sure that they are labelled and that the text is readable. If this is a problem, provide a handout with the diagram labelled effectively. When writing on flipcharts, make sure that you have a good-quality marker pen.

Practise

Write down the words you want to use to open your presentation. These might appear on your first slide. For example:

WELCOME – NAME – TITLE OF PITCH

Investigate using a range of fonts, sizes and word art to present the words as professionally as you can.

- Are the words clear?
- Are the words legible?
- Do the words impact on the audience?

Consideration of the needs and interests of the audience

Try to use a range of presentation methods so that all interests and preferences are catered for. For example, if you are using PowerPoint®, think about using a flipchart as well to highlight and expand on your points.

Clarifying technical aspects

Depending on your audience's knowledge, you might have to hand draw diagrams or make lists to explain and clarify technical aspects of your product or service. This will also show that you are adaptable to situations and are capable of using high-level communication.

It is important to check whether anyone in the audience has specific needs. This will show that you have prepared for a diverse audience and that you have considered the importance of meeting the needs of individuals.

Specific need	Solutions
Mobility impairment	• Ensure that tables are at the right height, there is space for a wheelchair or suitable seating • There should also be a person on hand for support
Hearing impairment	• Seating at the front, clarity of speech, printed handouts • Seated next to hearing person for support
Visual impairment	Large-print handouts, laptop with presentation at closer distance

Table 4.9: Thinking about the needs of audience members

Prepare for a diverse audience, allowing room for wheelchairs, for example, and encouraging anyone with visual problems to sit close to the front

Audience

Your audience might be made up of a diverse range of people.

Table 4.10: Types of people who might come to your presentation

Who	Role	Focus
The investor	Someone with money to invest, looking for opportunities to make a profit. Likely to be in business themselves, and may be involved in selling similar products and services.	Your financial information – cash flow, forecasts, planning and projected profits.
The bank manager	If you need a bank loan, they will want to know that your idea is sound and viable.	Like the investor, they will be interested in your financial information.
Suppliers	They would become stakeholders in your business, because they will provide the raw materials and services you need for the day-to-day running of your enterprise. Could be insurance brokers, office suppliers or transport companies.	They will be interested in what you have to offer them. Their businesses depend on new enterprise, and they will want your custom.
Business partners	If you are working with others to promote your idea, they will be in the audience. They will probably also contribute to your pitch. If active in the business, they might also have some responsibility for the content of your business plan. Or they could have invested in the business but want no part in the day-to-day management – often called 'sleeping partners'.	To support communication of the idea to the audience, to network with other members of the audience and to contribute to the question-and-answer session (particularly if they have specific, technical expertise).
Donator	Donations to business ventures are often given because the business has some ethical or charitable focus of interest to the donator. If your business idea involves supporting people with specific needs, or where need has been identified and is not supported by government funding, it is more likely that a donator will offer to help.	To examine the ethical and cultural aims of your enterprise to see if these meet their own aims for funding.

Skills and knowledge check

- ☐ What is meant by listening to understand a question?
- ☐ What are investors looking for in a pitch?
- ☐ Name three communication methods.
- ☐ Explain the difference between good and poor communication.
- ☐ Identify five key factors in presenting to an audience.

- ◯ I can use body language effectively when communicating.
- ◯ I can communicate confidently in a variety of ways.
- ◯ I can prepare the room for my presentation.
- ◯ I can identify the needs of the audience.
- ◯ I can answer relevant questions.

Link it up

In Unit 1 (A1) you explored different types of ownership and liability.

Ready for assessment

You will be expected to deliver a confident and well-structured pitch using your business plan from the previous learning aim in this unit. Your presentation will take place in front of an audience, who will ask questions about your plan. The audience should include a potential investor or business adviser.

For practice, you could work with colleagues and others to develop strategies to help you to develop a professional approach to your pitch.

You could develop a 'peer assessment form' and practise your presentation in front of your peers to get feedback.

Your assessment form could include the following statements:

CHECKLIST

- ☐ The presenter was appropriately dressed.
- ☐ The presenter spoke confidently about their product/service.
- ☐ The presenter showed a positive attitude and was professional in their approach.
- ☐ The presenter used technology effectively.
- ☐ The presentation was suitable for the audience.
- ☐ The presentation was delivered confidently.
- ☐ The content of the presentation was accurate.
- ☐ Questions were answered effectively.

At the end of your practice sessions, your colleagues or peers could give you oral and written feedback to help you to develop your presentation further.

C Review and revise the business plan to respond to feedback

C1 Using feedback and review to identify changes in a business plan

Before your presentation you will have the opportunity to discuss a range of feedback methods. These might include:

- feedback sheets from the audience, peers and/or colleagues.
- oral feedback from individual members of the audience.
- oral feedback from your mentor/assessor/colleagues.
- group feedback from a panel, colleagues.

Oral feedback has a more positive impact than written feedback because the observers can clarify their comments more easily and you can instantly get further information. Plan how you want to receive your feedback and the types of feedback you would prefer. If this is out of your control, think about how you feel about getting feedback and prepare yourself for how you might respond.

Receive feedback from the pitch audience

Whatever feedback method is used, your audience will be looking at two main aspects of your pitch.

The business content

The business content will cover everything that is in your business plan, including details of your product or service; market research; promotional plan; financial plan; risk analysis; and target setting.

The presentation skills demonstrated

The feedback on presentation skills will be based on your personal performance and will focus on presentation; behaviour and conduct; communication skills; and use of visual aids.

Using feedback from the pitch audience

Reflect on your own performance

Most observation or feedback sheets include a range of statements with space for the audience to make comments against each statement. The examples below show the difference between looking at the business content and the presentation skills demonstrated. Different members of the audience might give feedback on different aspects of the pitch.

Take time to analyse comments and think deeply about your performance. Consider how you can improve and develop your skills and knowledge further. You could:

- talk through your feedback with a mentor or coach
- keep a reflective journal
- work with a group to share your experiences
- compare your performance step-by-step against a 'model' performance.

STEP BY STEP REFLECTING ON YOUR PERFORMANCE

Follow the process

STEP 1

Identify the theme

☐ Choose a common theme from your feedback, for example an aspect of your presentation skills or use of technology.

☐ Make one specific goal an aim of the reflective process.

Example

I want to improve my confidence in delivering presentations.

STEP 2

Describe what happened

☐ Write in detail about how you felt and how your confidence stopped you from presenting effectively.

☐ Think about the specific problems, and be honest.

☐ At the end of the description, write a sentence stating what is stopping you improving your confidence.

☐ What are the barriers?

STEP 3

Think through solutions

☐ Think realistically about what you can do about the problem. You could write a bullet point list of what you could do to improve your confidence.

Example

- I could be better prepared.
- I could practise more in front of different audiences.
- I could observe others to give me some ideas.

STEP 4

Decide what to do

☐ Examine your list from Step 3 and think realistically about what you can achieve. Commit to doing something practically about your skills.

☐ Say exactly what you will do, when you will do it and what will be the first step.

Example

By the end of the month I will observe a presentation and talk to the presenter about how they gained the confidence to deliver.

The first step to doing this will be to contact my mentor to arrange the observation. I will do this today.

Reviewing audience feedback on the pitch

Giving and receiving feedback is a skill and can be difficult. Do not assume that everyone will know how to give it effectively. If feedback is given poorly, it could cause relationship problems in the workplace. See feedback as something positive that will help you to improve your business plan. Feedback should:

- be specific and relate to key points
- highlight what went well
- offer alternative solutions to problems
- help to develop ideas that are already in the pitch
- encourage you to take further actions.

Good feedback	Poor feedback
Is positive	Is personal
Is evaluative	Is negative
Is constructive	Patronises or is condescending
Supports further actions	Is vague
Is consistent	Is sarcastic
Gives encouragement	Leaves the presenter feeling de-motivated and possibly even wanting to give up
Leaves the presenter feeling positive and motivated to move forward	

Table 4.11: Helpful and unhelpful feedback

What if...?

Brenda and Bill have presented their new idea to management. Unfortunately, it did not go well. They were very nervous and felt that they did not perform as well as they could have. There was so much they missed out, and the result was that feedback from management asked for more detail. They felt very downhearted.

1 If you were their workplace mentor, what would your advice to them be?

2 If you were their manager, would you encourage them to do the presentation again?

3 If you were their colleague, what would you say to them for moral support?

Link it up

You will have looked at closed and open questions in Unit 2 (C2), when you looked at market research. Remind yourself of these question types when writing your feedback forms.

Evaluating feedback

Before you review the audience feedback, you will first need to evaluate it. Get as much detail recorded as possible so that you have enough information to evaluate effectively. For example, if you have organised a forum to discuss your presentation, it would be useful to record the discussion.

Feedback forms are the most common way of getting information, but they are not always useful if the forms do not ask **OPEN QUESTIONS** or allow enough space for the feedback. So it is important to plan how you want your feedback at the beginning of the process – to get the most information, the questions on your forms need to be open questions.

Breaking down feedback

When you have all the information in front of you, organise the detail of the feedback into sections. One way is to choose a series of headings – it will help if headings are already on the form. But if the feedback has been taken in a variety of ways, you will need to work out how to bring it all together in a consistent way. When the information is sectioned under clear headings, you can more easily identify recommendations for improvements to your business plan.

Try not to focus on any negative feedback – it will often be a small sample. Focus first on the positive comments and look for common themes.

Using feedback in your presentation

You could present your review in a paper or as part of a presentation. You can illustrate the results of the feedback using images, graphs and charts. This will help to show the percentages of the audience who identified gaps in your business plan or areas for development.

Some of the feedback will be about the business content and clearly identify where your business plan should be changed to improve your strategies, some will directly identify specific parts of your plan and some will be more complex and comment on a range of problems. Interpreting data and information can be difficult, so it might be useful to work as a group to help you to understand the best way forward.

Practise

What went well?

- Write down five positive feedback comments based on the business content of your pitch.

- Write down five positive feedback comments based on your presentation skills.

It would have been even better if...

- Write down two things that you would improve if you did the presentation again.

Determine required changes in the business plan

Remember that the feedback will be from a range of individuals. Although their views are important, you must identify what is useful for you as the business owner. Some of the feedback may not be relevant or appropriate to take your idea forward. You, as the entrepreneur, make the final decision about what goes into the final copy of your business plan.

Make your changes through an evidenced approach – think carefully about the impact of the changes you will make. You may have to compromise with investors. If someone is investing in or donating to your business, they may want to have their views taken into account.

Reflecting on your own skills

Identifying strengths and skills gaps

Gather the feedback that has identified your strengths and your skills gaps, and analyse it to reflect on your abilities.

You should feel more confident, having been through the processes of developing your business plan and delivering your pitch. Reflect on your progress to date. Analyse your strengths and skills gaps against a set of skills criteria.

Problem solving and communication	• Research skills • Presentation skills • Presenting documents
Management of information	• Calculating costs and revenue in the production of financial documents • Interpreting financial statements • Analysing information to identify required actions
Self-management and development	• Receiving feedback and evaluating it • Using that feedback to set new targets and amend content

Table 4.12: Identifying your own strengths and weaknesses

To support your reflection and target setting, you could use a **SWOT ANALYSIS** (strengths, weaknesses, opportunities, threats). Complete each point honestly and with as much detail as possible.

Setting goals and planning for their achievement

Consider preparing an action plan for your goals that you can work on. An effective working practice is to look again at your action plan at the end of each day to evaluate your progress and develop it as appropriate.

An action plan can take the form of a simple table with headings to suit your needs. For example:

Link it up

Look back at Unit 1 (B1) to remind you how to complete a SWOT analysis and consider how you would use it for the purpose of reflection.

What I need to do	**When will I do it?**	**Comments**
I need to do more presentations to gain confidence and improve my skills	Next week, I will present the review of my business plan	It went well, but I still need to do more. I am improving, but still nervous

Table 4.13: Developing presentation skills: action plan

More complex action plans might include headings such as:

• what resources do I need?
• who will help me?
• what are the constraints and what is stopping me?
• reflection
• improvements
• dates
• further actions.

You could use tick boxes to analyse your progress. You might also involve other people, such as mentors, line managers and colleagues in your action plan to get feedback.

Skills and knowledge check

- ☐ What is meant by reflecting on your performance?
- ☐ Name the four focus points in a SWOT analysis.
- ☐ Suggest five headings that you might find in an action plan.
- ☐ Explain the difference between an open and a closed question.

- ○ I can evaluate information from a variety of sources.
- ○ I can give and receive constructive feedback effectively.
- ○ I can analyse data.
- ○ I can set personal targets.

Ready for assessment

You will need to produce evidence of having analysed your business plan or enterprise idea, based on feedback on your own performance. You will also need to justify a set of recommendations.

Remember that when you are analysing, you need to make the point, explain the point and then expand on the explanation. It is not enough just to describe what has happened. You will also need to understand how to justify your choices. It is not enough to list suggestions for improvement, you will have to explain your reasons for making recommendations.

It will help to follow a process:

1 Organise the feedback (written, oral, mentor support, assessor support).

2 Refer to your reflective journal to evaluate the journey and the impact earlier learning had on your performance.

3 Highlight the main points using an analytical tool such as SWOT.

4 Critically evaluate/analyse your strengths and areas for improvement.

5 Discuss your first thoughts with a mentor, assessor, peer.

6 Write a reflective account of your performance based on your analysis (this might form part of a reflective journal).

7 Based on your findings, write a set of recommendations for improvement with an explanation of why the recommendations are valid, appropriate and relevant.

8 Adapt and revise the business plan to include the recommendations. The revisions should be based on self-reflection and feedback from others.

Self-evaluation

Have you:

- Synthesised the information from all feedback?

- Used analytical skill to critically evaluate your performance?

- Written or presented a full analysis of your findings, including a justification for recommendations?

- Adapted your business plan giving consideration to further support needed?

- Organised your evidence for assessment?

WORK FOCUS

HANDS ON

Problem solving is an important part of working life. In business you will come across a range of issues that need attention.

- Identify problems you can solve without requiring you to analyse your actions.

- Identify practical problems that simply require you to learn through practice or repetition. For example:
  - the technology is not working for your presentation
  - you have arrived at a venue to do a pitch and you have been given the wrong date
  - correcting errors in written work
  - computer problems.

- If possible, direct the problem to the relevant person who has responsibility for that working area (for example the Technical Department).

- Remember that it is not failure to ask for help.

- With difficult problems, work through a process:
  - identify the problem
  - describe the problem
  - explain issues within the problem
  - ask relevant questions to clarify information given
  - make realistic and appropriate decisions that will help to solve the problem
  - come up with creative and innovative ideas to solve the problem
  - show resolve and resilience in solving the problem.

- Develop your **BUSINESS ACUMEN** (a clear understanding of how your business works):
  - can be developed over time, because knowledge of working practices grows through experience
  - helps with problem solving and dealing with complex issues.

Ready for work?

How good are you at solving problems in business planning, pitching ideas and reflecting on your actions? Using the steps outlined in Hands on (above), and looking back through learning aim C, work through these scenarios to come up with solutions to the problems presented.

Table 4.14: Problems and solutions for business planning and pitching

Problem	Solution
Your mentor/supervisor thinks that your business plan needs re-formatting (you disagree).	
Your questionnaires from potential customers have come back with yes/no answers only, giving you very little data to work with.	
You have organised a launch event to promote your product or service and you sent out 200 leaflets, but only 10 people have accepted the invitation.	
The business location you have chosen is perfect, but you have just heard that another, similar business is opening two doors away.	
You have found out that a competitor is undercutting the price of your product or service.	
Your data analysis shows that your product or service is too expensive to produce.	
You have pitched your product or service to an audience and you did not do as well as you expected. You feel you could do better.	
The technology lets you down during your pitch.	
You have had feedback from your mentor/supervisor and you feel it is unfair.	
You do not understand how to evaluate, reflect and review but are too embarrassed to ask your supervisor for help.	

Glossary of key terms

AFTERSALES SERVICE: support that the business can offer to its customers

BALANCE SHEET: statement of financial position

BIASED: favouring one particular group or opinion

BRAND: a trademark or distinctive name identifying a product or service, often applied to a product or service that stands out in the market

BRAND VALUES: qualities that customers associate with the product or service

BREAK EVEN: the point at which the total cost of providing the product or service is equal to the income gained from selling it

BREAK-EVEN POINT: when the total revenue equals the total costs

BRICKS AND CLICKS: using both the internet and physical stores to sell products

BUSINESS ANGELS: people who will take shares in your business in return for providing funds

BUSINESS ACUMEN: a clear understanding of how your business works

BUSINESS ENVIRONMENT: the internal and external factors that influence a business

BUSINESS TO BUSINESS (B2B): a business that sells its product or service to other businesses

CAPITAL: the money, buildings and equipment used to run a business

CARBON EMISSIONS: harmful gasses produced during transport or manufacturing

CARBON FOOTPRINT: the amount of carbon dioxide that is produced by a business

CASH-FLOW FORECAST: a record of all the cash that has flowed into the business (inflows) and the cash that has flowed out of the business (outflows) in a given time period

CHARITABLE TRUSTS: organisations created with the purpose of being charitable to others and benefiting the public

CLOSED QUESTIONS: the type of question used to gather precise data, which will typically have 'yes' or 'no' answers

COMMUNITY INTEREST COMPANY (CIC): a special type of limited company that exists to benefit the community, instead of shareholders; it will aim to use its profits for good causes

COMPETITOR-BASED: before a price is set, the price of competitors' products or services is considered; this usually results in charging the same price as competitors

CONCEPT: an idea to help sell or promote a product or service

CO-OPERATIVE: an organisation formed when a group of people come together to work towards a common goal – co-operatives are owned and run by their members

COOLING-OFF PERIOD: the time within which the customer can change their mind and cancel the agreement

CORPORATE SOCIAL RESPONSIBILITY: the steps that a business takes to reduce the negative impacts that its activities have on communities and the environment

COST PLUS: calculating the break-even price for the product by adding material costs, direct labour costs and other expenses. Then, based on the profit the business needs to make, a percentage is added to this to calculate the final price charged to customers

CREDITORS: people or organisations that the business owes money to

CURRENT ASSETS: what the business owns on a day-to-day basis, including stock (raw materials and products), cash and money owed to the business by others (debtors)

CURRENT LIABILITIES: the amounts of money (liabilities) owed by the business to others that must be paid back within the next 12 months

CURRENT RATIO: a measure of how easily a business can pay off its current liabilities from its current assets, in other words how easily it can pay its short-term debts

CUSTOMER BASE: the type of customers you have

DEBTORS: people or organisations who owe the business money

DEMOGRAPHICS: the characteristics of human populations, for example the average age of a group of people

DIRECT MARKETING: marketing material sent directly to potential customers

ENDORSEMENT: a public show of approval or support for a product

ENTERPRISE: an organisation, large or small, that can either be run for profit or for social purposes

ENTREPRENEUR: someone who starts a business

EXECUTIVE SUMMARY: a short section at the start of a report that sums up the main points

FIT FOR PURPOSE: relevant to the customer base and designed to meet the needs of the target market

FIXED COSTS: costs that will not change, but are necessary for the business to run

FOUR PS: product, price, place and promotion – the main components of the marketing mix for a product or service

FRANCHISES: set up when the owner (franchisor) allows other people (franchisees) to use the name and the branding of an established business to set up a business of their own, effectively becoming an agent

GROSS PROFIT: calculated by subtracting the cost of sales from the sales revenue, i.e. the income from selling products minus how much they cost to make

GROSS PROFIT MARGIN: the gross profit as a percentage of turnover

HUMAN RESOURCES (HR): the people that work for or with the business to help it become successful

INCOME: the amount left when costs are taken away from revenue

INCOME STATEMENT: a document reporting the income generated by a business in a particular period of time, also called the profit and loss account

INSOLVENT: when a business is unable to pay debts

INTRAPRENEURSHIP: a new idea or revised idea within an existing business

JOURNALISTIC SIX: six questions (who, what, where, when, why and how) about an enterprise idea

LARGE ENTERPRISES: enterprises that have more than 250 employees

LATERAL THINKING: the ability to think creatively, or 'outside the box'

LEAD TIME: how long it will take for items to be delivered when an order has been made

LIABILITY: whether or not the owner of a business is personally responsible for its debts

LIFESTYLE BUSINESSES: set up to provide the founder with enough income to enjoy the quality of life they desire, as well as to provide flexibility

LIKERT SCALE QUESTIONS: respondents are asked to think about key factors of a product or service and rate them by order of preference

LIMITED LIABILITY: the owner is not personally responsible for any debts that the business has

LIMITED LIABILITY PARTNERSHIP (LLP): partners are not liable for any debts the business cannot pay

LIQUID CAPITAL RATIO (ACID TEST): a measure of a business's ability to pay off its current liabilities

LIQUIDITY: a business's ability to pay its debts

MARGIN OF SAFETY: the reduction in sales that can occur before the break-even point of a business is reached

MARK UP: the percentage that you are adding to the break-even cost of the product or service in cost-plus pricing. It ensures that a consistent level of profit is made

MARKET PENETRATION: increasing market share in the original market or entering new markets

MARKET RESEARCH: gathering information on potential customers, what they are likely to be able to pay for the product or service, and on potential competitors

MARKET SHARE: the proportion of the market dominated or controlled by a business

MARKETING MIX: the combination of product, price, place and promotion – this is also called the four Ps

MICRO: enterprises that have up to nine staff; they will usually be sole traders, partnerships or private limited companies

MIND MAPPING: ideas are organised into a diagram where they are placed in order or grouped under common headings

NET PROFIT: calculated by subtracting the total expenses from the gross profit

NET PROFIT MARGIN: the net profit as a percentage of turnover

NICHE MARKET: a small segment of the whole market that a product or service is focused on

NOT-FOR-PROFIT: enterprises that are formed to provide products and services free of charge; an example is the NHS

OPEN QUESTIONS: lets the respondents say whatever they like – the response to open questions can be long and detailed

OPERATING (RUNNING) COSTS: costs that are paid throughout the business's life

OPERATIONAL ENVIRONMENT: the internal and external factors that have an impact on the success of an enterprise

OUTFLOWS: the cash that has flowed out of the business

PARTNERSHIPS: businesses set up by two or more people, usually by professionals such as dentists, vets and accountants

PENETRATION PRICING: charging a low price initially, to encourage people to try the product and to establish brand loyalty; over time, the price is increased to make more profit

PESTEL ANALYSIS: an analysis used by a business to identify political, economic, social, technological, environmental and legal factors

PITCH: present your enterprise idea to an audience

POINT OF SALE: the location at which the customer pays for their product and/or service

PRIMARY RESEARCH: gathering new and unique research data yourself to answer a specific question

PRIMARY SECTOR: where raw materials are extracted and food is grown; examples include farming and mining

PRIVATE LIMITED COMPANY (LTD): usually small to medium in size and usually employ people other than the owners

PRIVATE SECTOR: the part of the economy run by private individuals or organisations, rather than the state

PROFIT: the money that a business makes once it has covered all its costs

PROFITABILITY: how much profit a business makes from sales of a product or service

PROFIT MARGIN: how much profit a business is making as a percentage of its whole income from sales

PROMOTIONAL: methods used by a business to promote and publicise their product or service to the consumer to increase sales and awareness

PROMOTIONAL PLAN: outlines the way in which a business will raise awareness of its product or service

PUBLIC LIMITED COMPANY (PLC): usually large enterprises, which tend to employ thousands of people and make large profits

PUBLIC CORPORATIONS: corporations owned by the government, for example the BBC

PUBLIC RELATIONS (PR): communication from a business to its audience (potential customers), which needs to create and maintain a positive image

PUBLIC SECTOR: enterprises that are owned and run, either fully or partly, by the government; they usually provide a service to a community

QUALITATIVE RESEARCH: measures how people feel, what they think and why they make certain choices

QUANTITATIVE RESEARCH: measures what people think from a statistical and numerical point of view

QUATERNARY SECTOR: provides information services to customers, such as information technology, consultancy, and research and development

QUESTIONNAIRE: a list of questions to find out people's opinions, and their likes and dislikes, about the product or service

RETAIL: selling small quantities to a customer who will use the product or service themselves; examples include shops and market stalls

REVENUE: the money a business makes from sales

REVENUE STREAMS: the ways your business will make money

SALES PROJECTIONS: an estimate of how much you expect to sell over a particular time period

SAMPLE: the people you ask to participate in your research

SECONDARY RESEARCH: using information previously researched by other people

SECONDARY SECTOR: uses the raw materials from the primary sector to transform these into products that are ready to be sold, for example car manufacturers

SEVEN PS: product, price, place, promotion, physical evidence, people and process

SHAREHOLDERS: people who invest in the business

SKIMMING: charging a high price initially, to skim off as much profit as possible; over time, the price is reduced

SMART: specific, measurable, achievable, realistic and time-bound targets

SMES: small to medium-sized enterprises – small enterprises have between 10 and 49 staff; medium enterprises have between 50 and 249 staff

SOCIAL CAPITAL: the connections between people and organisations, and the creation of mutually advantageous projects and outcomes

SOCIAL ENTERPRISES: set up to tackle social problems, or to improve people's lives or the environment

SOLE TRADERS: 'one-person' businesses, commonly known as being self-employed, such as small shop owners and taxi drivers

SPONSORSHIP: when a business gives money to a charity, sports team, hospital or other organisation it wants to be associated with; in return, the product or service will be promoted by the organisation

STAKEHOLDERS: the people, or groups of people, who are directly affected by, or have an interest in, a business

START-UP COSTS: costs that a business incurs in order to get up and running

START-UPS: new businesses, which are often small

STORYTELLING: verbalising your ideas – explaining to others exactly what you plan to do, how you are going to do it and what the outcome will be

STRAP LINE: a short phrase summarising a product or service

SUPPLY CHAIN: a sequence of events or processes that a business will set up and use to source materials or stock that it will manufacture or sell to the customer

SUSTAINABILITY: where a business offsets any environmental damage it causes

SWOT ANALYSIS: the strengths, weaknesses, opportunities and threats relating to an enterprise idea

TARGET MARKET: the type of customers you hope to attract

TERTIARY SECTOR: provides services such as transport, education and retail

TGROW: the topic, goal, reality, options and will of an enterprise idea

THIRD-PARTY WEBSITES: selling products to the customer via other business's websites, such as Amazon and eBay

TRENDS: patterns that can be mapped over time

TURNOVER: also known as revenue, is the income generated from making sales

UNIQUE SELLING POINT (USP): the factor, or factors, that make the product or service different to those of competitors, to make it stand out in the market

UNIT: each individual product that can be sold

UNLIMITED LIABILITY: the owner is personally responsible for any debts that the business has and may have to sell personal belongings to pay these off

VALIDITY: when the results of any test or survey are factually accurate and logical

VARIABLE COSTS: costs that will vary according to the business activity

VENTURE CAPITALISTS: investors that provide either capital or support to start-ups, for a stake in the business

VISION (OR MISSION) STATEMENT: statements that describe the aims, goals and aspirations of a business

VISUALISATION: a technique used to create an image of your final enterprise idea, involving visualising the idea from all angles

VOLUNTARY SECTOR BUSINESS: provides services or promotes a cause that benefits the public

WEBSITE: a convenient way to sell products directly to customers, without the cost of running a physical shop

WHOLESALE: selling large quantities to retailers that then sell the product or service on to customers

WORKABLE CASH FLOW: having enough money available to cover the day-to-day running of the business, such as wages, paying suppliers and other low-cost consumables such as stationery, postage and fuel for vehicles

WORKING CAPITAL (NET CURRENT ASSETS): the money that the business has available, or that it expects to have soon, which enables it to pay for day-to-day costs, such as paying staff wages or buying raw materials

Index